PERMANENT COLLECTION OF ITALIAN DESIGN

ON MY

Vespa

ITALY ON THE MOVE

curated by Pier Paride Vidari

CHARTA

Edizioni della Triennale
Fondazione
La Triennale di Milano
Viale Alemagna, 6
20121 Milan
tel. +39-02724341
fax +39-0289010693
www.triennale.it

Design
Mauro Panzeri, P.A. Zanini,
(GrafCo3)

Cover Design
Barbara Bonacina

Editorial Coordination
Filomena Moscatelli

Editing
Charles Gute

Translation
Karel Clapshaw

Edizioni Charta
via della Moscova, 27
20121 Milan
Tel. +39-026598098/026598200
Fax +39-026598577
e-mail: edcharta@tin.it
www.chartaartbooks.it

**Permanent Collection
of Italian Design**
series edited by Silvana Annicchiarico

ON MY VESPA
Italy on the Move
September 21 – December 18, 2005

Conceived and Coordinated by
Silvana Annicchiarico

Curator
Pier Paride Vidari

Exhibition Design
Nicola Marras, Carlo Fiorini,
Samuele Polistina

Graphic Design
Mauro Panzeri, P.A. Zanini, (GrafCo3)

Historical and Image Research
Ares Bolognesi
Gaia Milani

Editing
Elisa Testori

"Cuore di Vespa" video
Gian Piero Brunetta
and Mirco Melanco

Special thanks to
Tommaso Fanfani,
President of the Piaggio
Foundation,
and Chiara Mani,
Head of External Relations
of the Piaggio Historical Archive
and the Piaggio Museum.

Cover
Detail from calendar, 1951
© Archivio Storico Piaggio

Back Cover
Marina Abramović on a Vespa
© Alex Majoli by Contrasto 2006,
photo published in Vogue America,
November 2005, page 228

Flaps
Vespa 125, 1949
© Archivio Storico Piaggio

CONTENTS

Silvana Annicchiarico

A TALE OF TWO WHEELS

On a Vespa, people generally go about in twos. Of course you can ride a Vespa on your own: in the first episode of *Caro diario*, for example, Nanni Moretti uses it to meander around the streets of Rome in thoughtful solitude. But that is an exception, an example of a kind of self-sufficient exclusiveness. Unlike the bicycle—intended and designed for solitary pedaling—or the automobile—ideal for the displacement of sedentary groups— the scooter launched by Piaggio in 1946 seems to have been made especially to accommodate two travelers on its saddle: generally a *he* and a *she*. Right from the start, the design of this object collaborated with the customs and codes of conduct of the time in dictating the posture and proxemics of its riders: the person at the controls (usually the male) straddled the seat with his legs perpendicular to the shield and handlebars, while the passenger (usually the female) sat sidesaddle, leaning slightly forwards to place her arms round her companion's waist. Among the various reasons given for the success of this means of transport and its rapid and enduring ascent to the Olympus of Italian design cults, the fact that it can be used for *a couple's enjoyment* has almost always been ignored and underrated.

Yet it is a fact that calls for our closest attention. The Vespa actually brings bodies closer together. In the years immediately after the Second World War and during the long-drawn-out, demanding fifties it not only offered Italy an agile and very friendly instrument to make a reality of collective dreams of mobility (social as well as geographic and territorial) but also made it necessary for bodies to travel in an embrace, combining the aeolian intoxication of speed with the languid softness of physical contact. Two people sitting on the seat of a Vespa have to touch, they have to hold on to one another and *feel each other*: in the moralistic climate of the fifties, still dominated by a Spartanly prophylactic, prohibitionist idea and practice of the body, the Vespa unintentionally became a "sinful" object, an excuse for overthrowing interdictions and taboos, a dangerous temptation of the flesh. Paradoxes of mechanics, marvels of design.

Sixty years have passed since the first Vespas were sold, and the fascination that they exert remains unaltered. The world has changed, ways of traveling have undergone profound modifications, yet the scooter designed by Corradino D'Ascanio is still there, one of the most long-lived objects in the history of Italian design—nearly as long-lived as the *Moka Bialetti* coffee maker, and certainly more so than another cult item, the *Lettera 22*. Unlike the Olivetti typewriter, which proved unable to withstand the impact of new technologies, the Vespa succeeded in overcoming the inevitable obsolescence of user objects and establishing an image that is very trendy and really entirely representative of the *spirit of our time*. After the war, when Italian films were slow to celebrate the unlikely epic of the bicycle (and its thefts) as an emblem of the country's contradictions and aspirations, the Vespa embodied the desire for a carefree lifestyle and the latent dynamism of a society that found it hard to endure the austere poverty of the postwar years; nowadays, in our times of traffic jams and congested towns, the Vespa has become synonymous with quickness, independence and autonomy.

Devoting one of the exhibitions of the Triennale's Permanent Collection of Italian Design not to a *type* but to a single object such as the Vespa—with all the variations in form and technology that it has experienced over the course of time—means recognizing not only the excellence of its design and performance but also the paradigmatic value that this object has acquired in the non-linear history of the highly complex discipline of design. In the story of the Piaggio scooter there is really a convergence of the theme of industrial rationalization with the history of communication, advertising, imagery, customs, landscape, and mobility. The Vespa's long journey along the highways of the world and of Italy has constantly been accompanied by the hum of history: one has only to look at it with affection and attention to rediscover, deep down inside, a small part of our own lives.

Tommaso Fanfani

THE VESPA: FROM ITALIAN "RECONSTRUCTION" TO WORLDWIDE SUCCESS

Economic and production aspects of an original idea

At noon on April 23, 1946, a patent application was presented at the Florence Central Patent Office for Inventions, Models and Trademarks for a "Motorcycle with a rational arrangement of instruments and parts, with frame and mudguards combined and a cowl covering the entire mechanical part." Four drawings accompanied the documentation. This was the birth of a vehicle that wrote one of the most important pages in the dynamics of motorization in Italy and throughout the world. The Piaggio factory in Pontedera had previously produced trains, high-speed locomotives, powerful 1750-hp aeronautical engines, gigantic airplanes such as the *P108*—the four-engine aircraft that started to come off the production lines in March 1938—and variable pitch propellers, used in many airplanes made in Italy and elsewhere.

From those products they switched to a small, two-wheeled vehicle with a mere 98-cc motor. Why such a decisive shift in production? Why such a radical change?

The war was then in its final dramatic moments. The outcome seemed to have been decided, and orders in the aeronautical and railway sector dropped drastically. The number of workers at Pontedera fell from over ten thousand to a few dozen after the Allied bombardments and the mines of the German troops destroyed much of the plant. The management and offices were first transferred to other locations nearby, such as Cascina and Fornacette, but the engineers, administrative staff, and designers were then moved to Biella, far from the areas of bombing or occupation.

In the end, Italy was destroyed. A quarter of the wealth of the nation was lost; many cities and towns in the south central region were reduced to a pile of rubble; hunger, inflation, and unemployment were the real scourges of the postwar period. "If the Allies don't send us at least two hundred million kilograms of wheat," Ferruccio Parri said on

Radio Milan on July 9, 1945, "we will all die of hunger." Mobility regarding the transport of people and goods had to come to terms with ruined roads, blown-up bridges, and devastated infrastructures.

Enrico Piaggio—the son of Rinaldo, the founder of Piaggio & C., and responsible for the company's factories in Tuscany (while the other son, Armando, was responsible for the Ligurian factories in Genova Sestri Ponente and Finale Ligure)—understood the urgency of resuming production in order once again to become a source of income and wealth for the area. He saw the need to contribute to the recommencement of production in a ravaged land. The young entrepreneur realized the objective difficulties of competing with American manufacturers in the aeronautical sector. He saw the brilliance of his own engineers, especially Corradino D'Ascanio, and the technical ability of the workforce, but he had to contend with a total lack of raw materials and the inadequacy of the installations, as well as the absence of financial resources required for any attempt to compete in the sectors of powerful aeronautical engines and large aircraft.

During the German occupation Enrico Piaggio asked his people to study the problem of light transport, and during one of his frequent trips to Biella he saw one of the design team's first results: the *Paperino*, or *MP5*, a small, streamlined motorcycle. Supporting the idea but not the result, Enrico assigned development of the prototype utility motorcycle to his best engineer, Corradino D'Ascanio. D'Ascanio, a helicopter designer, was a very brilliant, versatile inventor, but did not like motorcycles: he considered them uncomfortable to ride, foresaw problems with punctures and the complexity of the controls for the rider, and found a variety of insurmountable obstacles to making an object that could be introduced easily and on a large scale. Enrico asked him to seek a solution that responded to the extraordinary nature of the situation, requesting a design in which the motor was concealed inside the body. D'Ascanio sat down at the drawing board "one Sunday," as he recalls, and within three months, working with a very small group of designers and technicians, he presented Enrico Piaggio with a new prototype, the *MP6*. It was completely different from the previous vehicle: like an airplane, the bodywork was self-supporting, light, closed, and resistant to buckling; the typical tubular structure of the motorcycle had disappeared; you could mount it comfortably, like sitting on a soft chair or

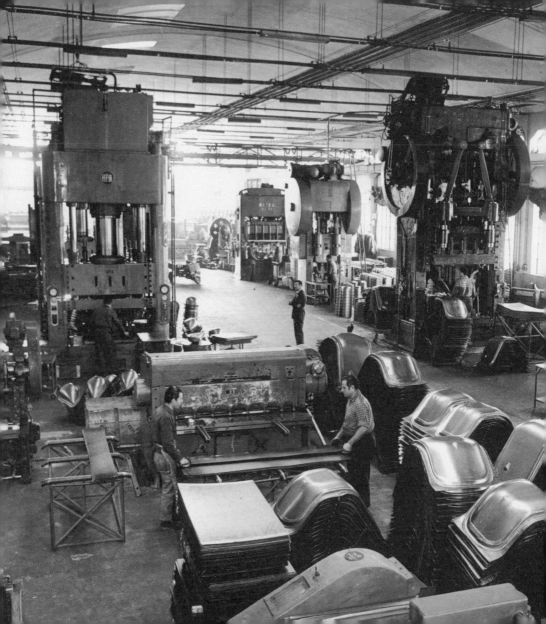

a lady's bicycle; all the controls were on the handlebars for easy use; the single-cylinder two-stroke engine was covered and formed a single unit with the rear wheel, without a chain or cardan shaft, and with the directly coupled gear system incorporated into the wheel-engine unit; the small wheels were concealed inside the mudguards; the wheels were suspended not from a fork but from a side arm, as on the front wheel of an airplane. Enrico Piaggio was ever-present in the design team's activity and D'Ascanio recalls that he was tenaciously critical and demanding. He was desperately keen to move on from the emergency situation of manufacturing saucepans (there was a market for kitchen equipment!) to a product consistent with the image and inherent value of a historic company that had been in the vanguard of innovation and technology ever since its creation in 1884; he wanted a product that could bring about a resumption of work in his factories and contribute to the country's reconstruction.

Enrico approved the *MP6* prototype and then very courageously set about manufacturing the first fifty Vespas. The name of the scooter came from an intuition that he had when he saw its special shape: "It has a narrow waist and a broad behind: *pare una vespa*—it looks like a wasp!"

The presentation of the product was prestigious. Although he had gone into production with the aim of achieving mass sales, Enrico Piaggio decided to show the Vespa in the refined, much-frequented setting of the Golf Club in Rome, in the presence of the highest civil, military, and religious authorities.

General Stone gazed curiously at the brand new vehicle tastefully colored in pastel green, posed beside the Vespa for the American Movietone newsreel, shook Enrico Piaggio's hand, and congratulated D'Ascanio and the engineers. The journalists present also looked at the Vespa with curiosity; some did not conceal—and subsequently reported—their doubts about its ability to hold the road or cope with hills, or, in short, to accomplish the manufacturer's avowed aim. Others were enthusiastic about its novelty and identified the Vespa as the first Italian postwar product, a kind of active demonstration of the desire for reconstruction transferred to a means of public transport—not unlike the Roman chariot had been, in the words of *Time* magazine. A flattering comparison.

Any technical doubts were rapidly dispelled by the road trials that the journalists themselves were allowed to carry out. Their reservations were replaced by the pleasurable surprise of riding on a vehicle that, despite its small dimensions and apparent limitation in terms of engine power, passed all tests, even the most severe.

In 1946 the Vespa was presented at the Milan Fair, as D'Ascanio recalls. With it was the *Ape* van, which was derived from the front part of the Vespa, had a rear platform capable of carrying 440 pounds, and could reach a speed of 25 miles per hour and climb 18% gradients fully loaded. The *Ape* went into production the following year, 1947. In addition to these first models of the utility van, a rickshaw version was also built for general use in big cities in China, to replace "pedicabs."

The first series of 50 Vespas went on sale at the end of April 1946: 48 vehicles were bought immediately, but two remained unsold until a couple of Piaggio engineers bought them to avoid "loss of face" for Enrico, who had so much faith in his product. Despite the modest success of these first 50 scooters, Enrico Piaggio showed courage, entrepreneurial spirit and farsightedness, and gave orders for the manufacture of 2484 Vespas.

The gamble paid off. Over the next few years there was an exponential growth in production, due, of course, to the extraordinary reaction of the public and the strategy employed for the marketing of the product. Among the first purchasers were entrepreneurs, aristocrats, and engineers. Among the nobility, Countess Negroni—a paradigm of female emancipation who rode a motorcycle and flew planes—helped to make the Vespa more widely known by organizing competitions for women and the "Three Seas Race," nourishing a contagious passion for the little vehicle.

Vespa Clubs were soon formed, races were organized, and the company started to produce racing models in 1947, progressing in 1951 to the *Vespa Siluro*, a small vehicle that was able to reach 107 mph in speed record trials.

This success was the result of the philosophy that had led to the birth of the Vespa: attractive design, a comfortable ride, great enjoyment for the user, flexibility and adaptability for all kinds of riders, safety, and low consumption.

But this success was also the outcome of the strategy of manufacturing, marketing, and communication.

Enrico Piaggio joined the system of assistance from the Marshall Plan and with the aid

provided bought a large press, an indispensable machine for making scooter bodies and coping with increasing demand for the product. As part of the training and exchange possibilities in the European Recovery Program, he sent engineers and mechanics to the United States to learn the most advanced strategies for the organization of manufacturing, marketing, and communication. The Pontedera factory was run by a former flying officer, Francesco Lanzara—a systematic person and a brilliant production manager.

The retail price of the Vespa—then about 65,000 liras—was high in relation to average salaries. The product was initially aimed at the upper-middle income bracket, and during the first few months the distribution was given to Lancia automobile dealers. But that stage did not last long.

To meet the increase in demand, Enrico Piaggio and his team decided to create a separate company to deal with Vespa distribution and wholesale. The result was Sarpi, under the direction of Umberto Barnato, which had the mission of optimizing promotion of the Vespa image and working out practical systems for sales and support.

On the communication front, advertising campaigns were soon launched, anticipating the designers' decisions and changes in language with the incisive introduction of themes such as women, young people, the environment, the economy, saving money, language, and aesthetics. The first calendars were published in 1953 and were distributed in various languages in many countries throughout the world.

The concern for the distribution network took on the characteristic dynamics of a modern company during a phase of recovery in the national economy. A network of dealers and Piaggio Service was quickly created, with a broad, extensive coverage attentively supervised by Sarpi.

On the international scene, in 1950 Piaggio started production of Vespas in Germany, with Hoffman-Werke in Lintorf. In 1951, licensees commenced activity in England (the Douglas Company in Bristol) and France (ACMA).

In 1953 production began in the Motovespa plant in Madrid. Within a few years of its appearance, the Vespa was being made in 13 countries and sold in 114 nations throughout the world, with over 10,000 sales and service points.

On the production front, after the first series in 1946, the following year saw the

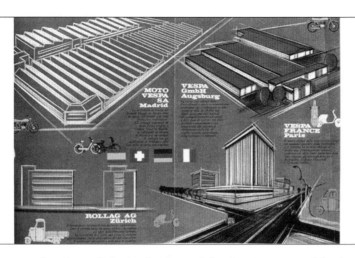

creation of the second series and the beginnings of the development of further models, so far totaling about 140.

In 1948 the *125* model was launched and immediately established itself, replacing the *98*. Made famous by the movie *Roman Holiday*, with Gregory Peck and Audrey Hepburn, the *125* wrote the first page of a long series of appearances of Vespas as "stars" in many celebrated films.

The *Vespa 125 U* model appeared in 1953; in 1955 there was the *Vespa GS*, the first model with a 150-cc motor, and the same year, at Pontedera, Corradino D'Ascanio designed the *Vespa 400*, a four-wheeled Vespa; 35,000 units of this small motor vehicle were subsequently made in France, in the Piaggio plant at Rochambeau.

The 50-cc model appeared in 1963; this new Vespa, needing no license plate, made its appearance at a point of crisis in the sector and proved to be an element of recovery and success. Constantly subjected to study and updating, many of the 140 models designed naturally remained as prototypes, whereas others, such as the *GS* (1955) and the *PX 125* (1977), were produced in millions.

The success of the Vespa can also be measured in the results reflecting production, financial position, and employment. The three diagrams that follow show the "Vespa

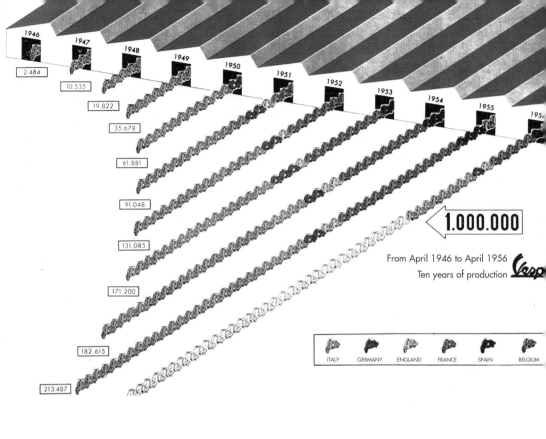

1946 2.484
1947 10.535
1948 19.822
1949 35.678
1950 61.881
1951 91.048
1952 131.085
1953 171.200
1954 182.615
1955 213.487
1956

1.000.000

From April 1946 to April 1956
Ten years of production *Vespa*

| ITALY | GERMANY | ENGLAND | FRANCE | SPAIN | BELGIUM |

effect." In the first, the production chart documents the achievement of the first million units produced by Piaggio at the Pontedera and Pisa plants and at the plants of licensees.

The Vespa effect can also be found on the balance sheet: after years of inactivity and serious losses in the final years of the war, Piaggio began to end the year with an increasingly satisfying financial position in 1947 and the following years. This result, expressed in terms of the prices prevailing at the time, documents the recovery and net financial improvement of the company.

Similarly, the number of white-collar and blue-collar workers grew consistently, as the table shows. Pontedera, a small town with fewer than 20,000 inhabitants, became a company town that developed around the Piaggio factory, a source of wealth, converting a predominantly rural society into a society of transformation.

Until 1967 the Vespa and Ape continued to be the two basic Piaggio products. They made the company's name great in the postwar period, determined its success, and contributed to wealth and productivity in Italy and in other countries, where there were still licensees.

In 1967, only a few months after the damage to the production lines caused by floods on November 4, 1966, the *Ciao* moped was launched on the market.

Since then, production has diversified. Vespa is still the leading and most enticing product, but other scooters and mopeds have joined the original "legend" and continue to

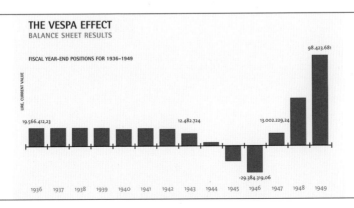

THE VESPA EFFECT
BALANCE SHEET RESULTS

FISCAL YEAR-END POSITIONS FOR 1936–1949

LIRE, CURRENT VALUE

19.566.412,23   12.482.724   13.002.229,24   98.423.681

-29.384.319,06

1936 1937 1938 1939 1940 1941 1942 1943 1944 1945 1946 1947 1948 1949

contribute to the greatness of a company that has written—and is still writing—one of the most fascinating pages in the great book of the metalworking industry in Italy and the world, and the great book of the history of entrepreneurship. Now that the last heirs of the Piaggio family have handed over their participation in the company (in 1999), a new entrepreneur and a new management have taken over the legacy of the 1946 Vespa, accepting the production challenge with the very same courage as was shown from the start, in a different world scenario now, though perhaps with complexities comparable to those of the early days from a market viewpoint.

Fifty years on from the creation of the *Vespa GS*, the *GTS* has been produced, technically a revolutionary vehicle in many respects, just as the 1955 model was a concrete sign of a renewed return to the strategic choices and business ability typical of the history of the name of Vespa.

There has been a continuity of innovation, people, and entrepreneurship that goes beyond any leap in time. Vespa is approaching the production milestone of 20 million vehicles. This is a flattering and significant outcome; it is the result of a long tale consisting of periods of growth and periods of crisis; but above all it is a result that has had—and still has—a constant need for managerial ability and entrepreneurship. This, I believe, is the challenge that Vespa has always faced, from Enrico Piaggio in 1946 to Roberto Colaninno in 2005. It is still a "vehicle" for economic growth; an evolutionary milestone for customs, communications, commercial strategies and modes of thinking; an instrument of social and civil change in a nation and an economy; and a guiding star that an attentive observer must have the ability to understand and follow.

THE VESPA EFFECT

NUMBER OF EMPLOYEES
AT THE PONTEDERA PLANT, 1945 TO 1961

YEAR	FACTORY	OFFICE	TOTAL
1945	60	30	90
1946	700	100	800
1947	1300	150	1450
1948	1760	245	2005
1949	2350	399	2650
1950	3000	320	3320
1951	3200	350	3550
1952	3484	399	3873
1954	3383	456	3839
1957	4046	532	4580
1958	4374	563	4937
1959	4530	604	5134
1960	4610	621	6231
1961	4870	658	5528

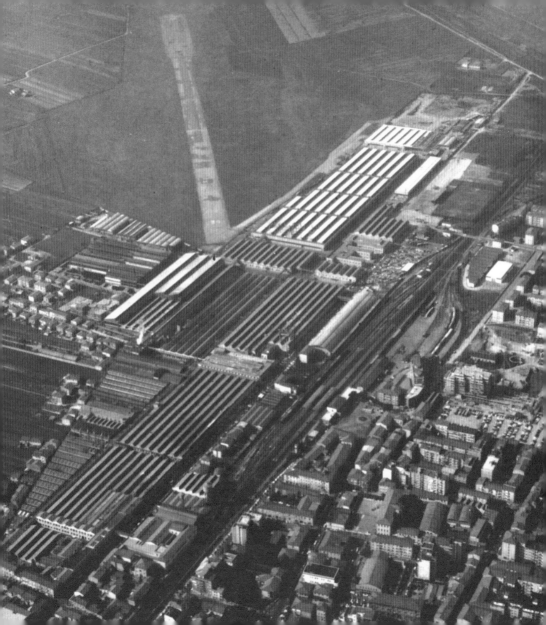

Pier Paride Vidari

FROM VESPA TO VESPA

Industrial design and product identity

INDUSTRIAL DESIGN

The birth of the Vespa was a design event marked from the outset by the typical logic of mass production, in which the key professional figure was the engineer.

The particular interest for the world that Piaggio represents in the area of Italian design has to do, therefore, with the analysis of a case in which what was needed was the design ability of someone who could not afford to conceive a handcrafted product, however brilliant and ingenious (with limited production possibilities and therefore fewer risks), contrary to what happened in other economic sectors in Italy.

Any mistake could have proved very costly and had a dramatic outcome for the whole company, whose production resources, workers, engineers, machines, systems, production plants and locations were—and still are—often very much bound up with work on a new project.

Vehicles are a particular field of application of the planning method that is now generally called design. It would be better to say "industrial design," taking in the activity of design but also placing emphasis on the adjective "industrial," that is, design for industry. In Italian universities these studies used to be classified under architecture, with the name of "artistic design for industry," perhaps to specify design with strong aesthetic connotations, distinguishing it from the attention to functionality typical of engineering.

The situation has now evolved into specific subjects and specializations. There is a relationship with objects and surroundings that is expressed in accordance with criteria drawn from an extensive combination of many different types of techniques, in terms of professional practice and training.

MINISTERO DELL'INDUSTRIA E DEL COMMERCIO

Ufficio Centrale dei Brevetti per Invenzioni, Modelli e Marchi

Brevetto per modello industriale

Brevetto per modello
utilità

N. 25456

DI BREVETTO

Firenze £.100
21/4/46

Questo Ufficio dà atto che concede il brevetto per il modello industriale quale appresso, come da domanda contraddistinta nel relativo Registro ed n. 70...

Ufficio di deposito: Firenze
Data ed ora di deposito: 21 Aprile 1946, ore 12
Titolare del brevetto e suo domicilio: Piaggio & C.Società per Azioni
a Genova

Titolo del modello: Motocicletta a complesso razionale di organi ed elementi con telaio combinato con parafanghi e cofano ricoprenti tutta la parte meccanica.

Il titolare ha dichiarato che, a norma delle Convenzioni internazionali vigenti, intende far valere, per il deposito italiano, il diritto di priorità derivante dal corrispondente primo deposito estero di cui appresso:

(Estremi della domanda e del brevetto di primo deposito all'estero): ///

Il presente brevetto, che viene comunque senza preventivo esame della novità del modello accordato, non garantisce che il modello medesimo abbia i caratteri voluti dalla legge perché il brevetto sia valido ed efficace.

(Annotazioni speciali): ///

Roma, li — 9 NOV 1946

IL DIRETTORE

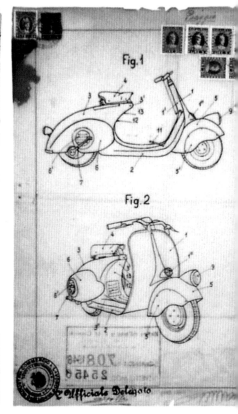

Fig. 1

Fig. 2

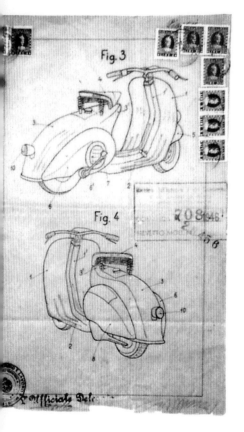

Fig. 3

Fig. 4

708

BREVETTO MODELLI

L'Officiale Del...

Descrizione del modello di Utilità avente per tito-
lo "MOTOCICLETTA A CONPLESSO RAZIONALE DI ORGANI
ED ELEMENTI PER TELAIO CARENATO, CON PARAFANGHI E
COFANO NASCONDENTI TUTTA LA PARTE MECCANICA" per
la P I A G G I O e C. Società per Azioni a
GENOVA.

Il modello riguarda una speciale forma di motocicletta alla quale si è accoppiare una adatta sa-
goma con razionale disposizione di elementi compo-
nenti il telaio, ed aventi la funzione di pedana,
parafanghi, cofano e speciale riparo anteriore a
forma arcuata; il tutto così conformato e combinato
da far risultare coperti e protetti tutti gli organi nascosti, e pratica e comoda la sistemazione del
motociclista.

Il modello è mostrato in via schematica dagli
annessi disegni nei quali la

Fig. 1 mostra la motocicletta completa in vista di fianco; la

Fig. 2 la mostra prospetticamente vista per
davanti; la

Fig. 3 la mostra sempre prospetticamente vista
di fianco; e la

Fig. 4 prospetticamente vista per di dietro.

La motocicletta è portato da un telaio compren-

- 1 -

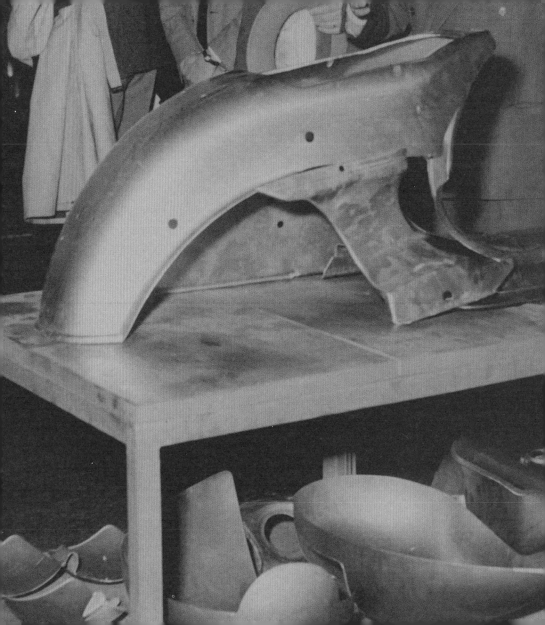

The world of vehicles—and particularly of automobiles—seems impervious to those that do their training in university lecture halls, instead preferring the sort of self-training that has produced the great Italian car body designers, who have gone on to become all-around designers. There are various reasons, including economic ones, to explain this situation, but there is no need to go into them here. However, this general practice provides a further point of interest for an appreciation of what went on in the Piaggio factories and in other Italian companies where, alongside the masterly treatment of the engineering side, the aesthetic aspect was never neglected either consciously or unconsciously.

Which is tantamount to saying that this sensibility is an intrinsic characteristic in the Italian way of designing and making objects.

EARLIER SCOOTERS

In 1894 the German company Hildebrand & Wolfmüller had already produced a bicycle with a motor and an open frame. However, the first real scooter was created in England and was made by Skootamota: it had a 124-cc 4-stroke engine and could reach a speed of 28 mph. Skootamota also produced the *ABC*, designed by the engineer Grandville Bradshaw, with a 125-cc 4-stroke engine and a speed of 25 mph.

After the appearance of the French *Le Touquet* at the start of the twenties, the *Unibus* was produced by Gloucestershire Aircraft in Cheltenham between 1920 and 1922, and in the thirties the Americans marketed the *Motor Glide*, with automatic transmission, covered engine, and front braking. We must also remember the American *Cushman 52*, nicknamed the "milking stool," made by the Cushman Motor Company in Lincoln, Nebraska, using pressed metal.

In Turin, in Italy, the *Velta* was created in 1938, designed by the engineer Vittorio Belmondo for Fiat.

All these models were basically designed to have the feet resting on a platform, with the engine at the back.

1945 - MP5 "paperino"

Drawing inspiration from the British and American scooters that he had probably seen as equipment issued to British paratroopers, Enrico Piaggio thought of the possibility of manufacturing a small motorcycle. It was to be interpreted not as a military vehicle or a plaything but as a general means of transport.

The assignment was initially given to an engineer called Spoldi. Because of the German occupation of the Pontedera factory, the technical and administrative offices had been transferred to Biella, where Piaggio had started making a small quantity of aluminum saucepans. After the transfer the Piaggio designers visited the castle of Count Trossi, well known as a racing-car driver at the time, who had collected a certain quantity of *Volugrafo* vehicles, obtained from a bankruptcy. It was at this point that the designers came into contact with the reality of the scooter and tried to develop the design of the *MP5*.

Renamed the *Paperino* (the Italian name for Donald Duck), the *MP5* had a 98-cc engine with a maximum speed of 22 mph and two gears. The large front mudguard enveloping the wheel, with the headlight embedded above it, also had a load-bearing function and replaced the fork. The saddle-shaped structural body supported the seat. The vehicle had a Sachs engine, the same as the one fitted on the *Velta* scooter designed by Belmondo, with a chain drive. There are some *MP5* scooters with an engine marked as Piaggio, but the technical characteristics are those of the Sachs engine. The rider of the *MP5* sat astride the seat in the traditional manner. The design was proposed in 1945 but was not approved by the management.

1946 – *Vespa 98*

The company then turned to the engineer Corradino D'Ascanio, a brilliant aeronautical designer, who asked for and obtained carte blanche for the design. D'Ascanio had no experience of designing motorcycles but he created a revolutionary vehicle, seemingly based on an indifference to the general practice normally shown in motorcycle designs.

Enrico Piaggio himself gave the name of Vespa to the new small motorcycle, perhaps because of its slender waist, perhaps because of the pointed abdomen of the prototype or the handlebars that looked like antennae, or perhaps from the idea of swarms of speedy scooters whizzing along the roads of Italy.

The *MP6* appeared, followed by the *Vespa 98* (98 cc), and the event was announced by the *Corriere d'Informazione* on March 29, 1946. The vehicle exuded elegance and, as D'Ascanio said, it was not at all like a noisy, uncomfortable motorcycle. Although the first 50 vehicles were made at Biella, the first 15 scooters of the official production came from the Pontedera factory, and a presentation was organized at the Golf Circle in Rome, in the presence of General Stone of the US Army. After the first units, thousands more were manufactured.

It was a vehicle with a pressed steel, monoshell, load-bearing frame and a handlebar gearshift. The engine was air-cooled and positioned on the right of the rear wheel. The cover was similar to the shapes used in aeronautical design, fixed by insertion of the upper edge into a channel with a rubber fitting. The arm supporting the front wheel was derived from an airplane undercarriage and made it easy to change the wheel. Another feature was the protective shield, with a bulge where the monotube support with the wheel was inserted. All the controls were on the bicycle-style handlebars, including the three-speed gear lever: this arrangement made the scooter easier to handle. This model was not fitted with a stand, but instead had two light alloy semicircular pieces fixed to the platform, which supported the weight of the vehicle when it was leaned sideways.

On April 23 of that year an application was lodged for an industrial patent for a vehicle "with a rational arrangement of instruments and parts, with frame and mudguards combined and a cowl covering the entire mechanical part." In the designer's description, attention was clearly paid to the aesthetic aspect: "… although the overall design corresponds to a comfortable, rational motorcycle with protection from mud and dust, as can be seen from the drawings and as also indicated in the description, nevertheless the requirements of aesthetics and elegance are also preserved."

At the end there was a somewhat modest comment that the vehicle was "a non-ornamental, utility model." The patent was granted on November 9, 1946.

The company decided to mass-produce about 2000 of these scooters, and the model remained in production until 1947, with four slightly different series resulting from the

1946 - VESPA 98

1949 - VESPA 125

gradual introduction of improvements. Some of the alterations were aimed at reducing the number of pieces and the comparative complexity of the product.

The Vespa proved reliable and extremely economical. The maximum cruising speed could be kept up over long distances, as the first users demonstrated, with improved averages on medium-to-long distances, on a par with light motorcycles and even with medium-sized engines. It boasted a top speed of 25–30 mph.

1948 – *Vespa 125 V1T*

A new, more powerful model was presented at the beginning of 1948, the *Vespa 125*, which immediately made a name for itself and soon replaced the *Vespa 98*. It was extremely successful and was produced in large quantities, with some improvements, including a complete rear suspension, consisting of a spring and hydraulic shock absorber. It also had a new style of handgrip, with the Piaggio mark repeated on the shield at the front, which also bore the name "Genova." Initially it had a large air intake to improve engine cooling and access, and the design was altered slightly, with the front mudguard also serving as the support for the headlamp, but in 1953, after numerous developments, the *Vespa 125* went back to having the engine and rear wheel completely covered, as in the original models, while the front headlamp remained on the front mudguard.

Production

The number of *Vespa 98* scooters produced was 2484 in 1946, 10,535 in 1947, 19,882 in 1948, and 35,000 by the end of 1949. A further 60,000 were produced in 1950, coinciding with the start of production by the first Piaggio "licensee" in Germany.

In 1953 171,200 Vespas were made, and from 1955–56 production reached 1,000,000. The event was recorded by the issue of a commemorative postage stamp.

From 1946 to 1965, the year of Enrico Piaggio's death, 3,350,000 Vespas were made in Italy, almost one for every 52 inhabitants.

In 1947 the *Ape* (Bee) appeared, a sort of development from the Vespa, setting the seal on the company's success in the utility vehicle sector.

That year Innocenti launched the Lambretta, a formidable competitor, but with a

1951 - VESPA 125

structure consisting of a single tubular girder, and therefore with a conception that was basically the opposite of the Vespa.

THE DESIGNER: CORRADINO D'ASCANIO (1891–1981)

A few lines must be devoted to the extraordinary personality of the Vespa's designer. Corrado (Corradino) D'Ascanio was born in Popoli (then in the province of L'Aquila, now in Pescara) on February 1, 1891. Even as a child D'Ascanio had been keen on flying, as he himself commented on various occasions: he studied how birds flew and the proportions between their weight and wingspread. He also made a glider, constructed with simple materials by he and his cousins, and he accomplished his first flights, leaps of a few dozen yards, from a hill. After attending the "Ferdinando Galiani" school in Chieti, in 1914 he graduated in mechanical industrial engineering from the Polytechnic University in Turin.

The war years

That very year he enlisted as a volunteer in the "Aviators' Battalion" of the Engineers' Corps in Turin, where he was initially assigned to testing engines. On March 21, 1915, he was sent to France as a second lieutenant in the Engineers' Reserve; he selected an engine to be manufactured in Italy and started production of La Rhône engines. After a brief flying course in a *Farman 14*, he was sent to the front, where he concentrated on maintaining equipment (he brought back into service about fifty *Caudron* airplanes, grounded because the lubricating oil had frozen, by devising a system for heating the engines).

In June 1916, while on temporary leave, he worked in the Technical Office of the "Società Anonima per Costruzioni Aeronautiche ing. Ottorino Pomilio & C.," which specialized in the construction of military aircraft such as the *SP2, PC, PD*, etc. There he took part in the construction of numerous prototypes of fighter planes and bombers.

Other inventions

We must mention the grant of his patent no. 32500, dated June 30, 1916, to the Pomilio

PIAGGIO & C.

GENOVA

COSTRUZIONI
IN ACCIAIO INOSSIDABILE

company in connection with the invention of a "universal automatic clinometer for airplanes and the like," which provided planes with an automatic indicator of longitudinal and lateral inclination.

He also worked on a fighter plane that had a speed of 148 mph, carried out the first installation of a radio-transmitting apparatus on an Italian aircraft, and tested a patent for an autopilot in a *Farman* plane.

Work in the United States

In January 1918, D'Ascanio traveled to the United States as technical secretary to Ernesto Pomilio, managing director of Pomilio Brothers Corporation, an aeronautical company based in Indianapolis, with which D'Ascanio collaborated until March 1919. In the United States, D'Ascanio also worked with Ugo Veniero D'Annunzio, Gabriele D'Annunzio's son, a designer in the Technical Bureau of Construction of Caproni Aeroplanes in Detroit, where the *Liberty Caproni* was being built, defined by D'Ascanio himself as "the most powerful terrestrial machine flying in the USA." Together with D'Annunzio he designed a private single-seater with a 20-hp Harley Davidson engine, and a flying boat, an amphibious single-seater with a 45–50-hp engine which he also tried to put into mass production.

The return to Italy

By this time production for the war had ended. Not finding a job in the American aeronautical industry, in 1920 D'Ascanio returned to Italy and set up a technical studio in Popoli.

In 1924 he designed a bomber plane and offered it to the Ministry of Aviation, but it was rejected. In the twenties and thirties D'Ascanio designed and lodged patents for various inventions, in the field of aviation or other areas, including the "automatic regulator for aviation engines" and the "aerial bomb that explodes at a predetermined height above the target."

His greatest love was designing helicopters.

On April 7, 1925, he applied for a patent for a "helicopter with two coaxial rotors with automatic descent mechanism." That year he had set up a company for the development

of "aviation industries in Abruzzo" with Baron Pietro Trojani, who invested all his assets in the enterprise. D'Ascanio designed a helicopter, applied for a patent for it, and had it made by the Campione foundry in Pescara. He was allowed to take part in the helicopter competition announced by the General Directorate of Engineering and Aeronautical Construction, but the project was presented outside the terms that had been established.

The first prototypes of the *D'AT1* and *D'AT2* (*D'AT* standing for D'Ascanio-Trojani) were soon presented. The *D'AT2* had a rigid articulation for the rotor blade and this led to the destruction of the prototype and the injuring of Trojani. The third prototype, the *D'AT3*, was commissioned by the Ministry of Aviation and was built in the airship hangar at Ciampino airport in Rome: it was piloted by Marinello Nelli.

The *D'AT3* was the first maneuverable helicopter in history. With rotors mounted on cardan joints, it flew at Ciampino in October 1930, setting records for flight time (8 hours and 45 minutes), altitude (57 ft), and distance flown (3,589 ft in a straight line) that remained unbeaten for years. A letter of congratulation from Giovanni Agnelli, regretting that he had been unable to witness the event, has been preserved.

D'Ascanio did not obtain a contract for mass production of this helicopter, perhaps because of rivalry between the Navy and the Air Force. The D'Ascanio-Trojani company came to the end of its financial resources and was dissolved in 1932 while the engineer was designing a variable pitch propeller.

In 1932 the young Enrico Piaggio, who had been running the Pontedera factory for four years, not only wanted the aeronautical designer but also acquired the patents for the variable pitch propellers. He called on him first as a consultant and then offered him a permanent post.

The first assignment on which D'Ascanio collaborated was the production of the *P16* bomber, to which a variable pitch propeller was applied. In 1936 D'Ascanio designed an auxiliary control circuit for anti-aircraft fire that was tested successfully at Sabaudia (Latina). In 1939 Enrico Piaggio approved the construction of further helicopters designed by D'Ascanio, such as the *PD1*. The *PD2* was not finished until 1943, but the prototype was destroyed in the bombing. The *PD3* originated as a successor to the *D'AT3*, revolutionary in form and perfectly functional in terms of performance, and it is still an object of wonder in comparison with modern helicopters. The first flight did not take place until 1942, when the *Sikorsky* was already flying for the Army in the United States. After the armistice (September 8, 1943), with the Pontedera factory mined by the Germans and bombed by the Allies, the Piaggio company moved to Biella.

As a result of this situation, D'Ascanio has never been named among the best-known aircraft designers, such as the British designers Mitchell, Handley Page, and De Havilland, the Dutch designer Fokker, the Russians Yakolev, Mikoyan, and Tupolev, the German Heinkel, the American Douglas and many others, although in 1948 he was co-president, together with Sikorsky, of the fourth annual Forum of the American Helicopter Society in Philadelphia, where he was hailed as a true pioneer.

We have already spoken of the events that led D'Ascanio to take over the design of the new scooter in 1946. When he arrived in Biella he found the enthusiasm there contagious. It was a challenge: in order to give the Italians two-wheeled transport, but with a different, original design that could not be assimilated with that of the ordinary motorcycle, D'Ascanio wanted to design in a nontraditional way, and he wanted carte blanche. Once approval had been obtained, he acted very quickly. Aided by the trusted designer Mario D'Este, he took only three months to design and build the prototypes. When he returned to Piaggio, D'Ascanio continued to work on alterations to the design of two helicopters, and in 1952 he got the *PD4* in the air, but it was no longer competitive: in fact the United States, with Sikorsky, had made great technical progress in this sector. The *PD4* was a three-seater, "with synchronized, twin-bladed, counter-rotating rotors arranged in tandem." During the final adjustments, however, there was an unexpected accident, and Enrico Piaggio stopped the experiments. It was 1951. By then 300,000 Vespas had been manufactured.

In 1964, after leaving Piaggio, D'Ascanio became a consultant to the Agusta group in Cascina Costa di Samarate (Varese), the leading Italian manufacturer of helicopters, with the idea of returning to Piaggio when the company resumed manufacture of helicopters.

In 1969 he designed a small training helicopter, the *ADA*, that could also be used for agriculture, but Agusta showed no interest in manufacturing it.

D'Ascanio died in Pisa on August 6, 1981. During his long life he received many

tributes and awards, such as the distinction of Knight of the Grand Cross presented by the Italian President, and all kinds of diplomas from aeronautical associations.

He wrote numerous scientific publications, published between 1954 and 1980, and he taught Machine and Project Design at Pisa University from 1937 (when he was working for Piaggio) to 1961.

FORM

All the Italian designers in the period immediately after the world war looked to Europe for experiments with the form of objects. They sought either to rediscover a legitimization of their own way of working or to find a new awareness of themselves in the international debate, becoming increasingly conscious of the importance of designing objects, goods and structures with moral and political continuity, an attitude that originated in the modern movement, especially in German rationalism, and that did not fail to admire the original personality of Le Corbusier.

In the north of Italy, especially, the influence of the Bauhaus provided models that were quickly interpreted with great originality. Almost all the designers, with a few particular exceptions such as Carlo Mollino, soon abandoned forms derived from Cubism in favor of softer forms, also described as "sculptural" forms, previously unthinkable but undoubtedly forming part of the modern movement and its subsequent evolution.

At the same time, as a result of American influence, everybody was dreaming of those marvelous kitchens over the ocean, with their huge refrigerators—not widely available in Italy—and other electrical appliances, enormous automobiles and gleaming, growling motorcycles, airplanes, and the whole wide world of wonders portrayed in the movies.

One could say that the great inventiveness of the Vespa was its shape, because of its originality in comparison with foreign scooters, and that its shape was possible because of the manufacturing technology selected and the very Italian idea of wanting to avoid imitation, even though similar rounded, functional forms had already been present before the war. We could cite various types of tram designed by the Municipal Tram Company in

Milan around 1932, the experimental *Dymaxion* vehicle designed in 1933 by Buckminster Fuller, or the *Mallard* locomotives designed by Sir Nigel Gresley in 1935.

We must also certainly mention the Volkswagen *Beetle*, designed by Ferdinand "Ferry" Porsche between 1935 and 1938 and supported by the regime, and the radio receiver designed for Phonola by Luigi Caccia Dominioni, and Livio and Pier Giacomo Castiglioni in 1940. These are just a few of the many examples that show a trend.

Le Corbusier also revealed a similar attitude in the Notre-Dame-du-Haut chapel at Ronchamp, with forms definitely closer to a large sculptural work than to the ways of rationalism, for example in the elegant yet powerful curvature of the walls and roof. Le Corbusier found the maximum expression of the potentials of construction, offering an extraordinary, changeable form very far from the Cubist "purity" of other famous figures of the time.

In Italy, a particularly important figure in the exploration of form was Marcello Nizzoli, originally a painter and sculptor and later a designer, who was born in Boretto (Reggio Emilia) in 1887 and died in Milan in 1969.

In Milan he became interested in industrial design as a result of his contact with Persico, Terragni, and others. Although the influence of rationalism, or even Central European Neo-Plasticism, is clearly visible in the Parker premises in Santa Margherita square in Milan, designed in conjunction with Persico in 1934, it was after he met Adriano Olivetti that Nizzoli resumed his study of increasingly sculptural, plastic forms for industrial products.

In 1940, the Olivetti *Summa 40* adding machine marked the beginning of a prodigious activity that was crucial for the maturity of Italian design. Later, with the Olivetti *Lexikon 80*, and with the *Lettera 22* in 1946/48, it achieved what was possibly its greatest and most harmonious expression. In these cases Nizzoli integrated all the most strictly functional, mechanical parts of the object in a formal unity that did not neglect ergonomic aspects.

The product thus acquired a unified appearance of obvious functionality and easy legibility, as with the Vespa. It has often been said that D'Ascanio's design for the Vespa was derived from the typical structural principles of aeronautical manufacturing of the

1947 - VESPA 98 CORSA

1945 - MP6

time: for example, one can see in it references to the Savoia Marchetti aircraft of 1922.

The streamlining of the combination of engine, rear wheel, and seat that resulted from this influence offered a "thick wing" profile, with a soft, rounded shape that was also flowing and aerodynamic, a feature already present in some automobiles of the forties.

The aim was to conceal the internal complexity and contain as many parts as possible in the bodywork, modeling the whole as a "single volume" that also included the mudguards. The design conveyed an aerodynamic feeling and gave a very assured image, concentrating the weight at the rear.

Seen from the side, the Vespa is elegantly slender at the front, completed by a large mudguard. If one looks carefully at the shape from the side, the rear part, containing the engine and the back wheel that supports the seat, provides a "filled space" that contrasts with the "empty space" of the front part and the footrest.

A filled space and an empty space, one positive and the other negative, with similar volumes. The two volumes have almost identical dimensions, measured from the main axis of the machine, equal to about 25 inches. A strong sense of proportion, pursued and maintained, that immediately brought admiration and success. An overhang was provided by the position of the seat, projecting above the hollow of the footrest, and the handlebars, "detached" from the shield.

For large or small motorcycles, the principle of containing everything inside a single housing and concealing the engine and transmission was not usual; instead, they tended to consist of frames on which the various mechanical parts were placed or inserted. This choice proved to be an excellent strategy and at the same time it gave the product a shape that was unique in terms of originality and consistency, completely adopting the principle and obtaining a "total" form.

The electrically welded, pressed steel body was subsequently considered the indispensable characteristic in the entire evolution of the Vespa in years to come.

The rear tip, holding the license plate and taillight, suggests a biological reading of the object: immediately identified as resembling the abdomen of an insect—a wasp, to be precise—it was subsequently seen by the public as a female form.

At the front there is the elegant ribbing of the steering column. The front part is characterized by the rather high shield and the headlight, although with variants in terms of its position. The shield provides the rider with protection against collisions, and also from dust and weather, and it supplies a visible psychological reference, previously not considered in the customary formal canon of the motorcycle.

The front wheel, although provided with a cover that changed with time, and with a suspension clearly derived from aviation, gives a further recognizable characteristic, confirming the general line.

The great accessibility, aided by the seated rather than straddling position, ensures comfort, but the more upright posture of the rider is less aerodynamic. The asymmetry of the weight at the rear, due to the side position of the engine, caused considerable problems, especially in maneuverability, which had to be maximized.

Meanwhile, the companies that manufactured vehicles, especially Fiat, which had also emerged from the vicissitudes of autarchy and war, had been obliged to change their installations and reconsider the evolution of vehicle engines and bodies. Those models of wartime production that had not been destroyed had become obsolete.

There was an intuition of the need to respond to the demand for private transport for people and goods, aimed not only at simple needs but also at a renewed desire for movement, abandoning the train, the traditional form of transport for the masses.

COLORS

In the period preceding the Second World War, the objects that had been launched on the market—whether items for work or vehicles—had been almost exclusively black in color, probably because of the conviction that, if dark colors such as black or deep brown were adopted, dirt and oil stains would be less evident.

Colors changed quickly when the war ended. Cubism and rationalism, influencing industrial design and manufactured objects, suggested the possibility of considering warm white colors, light grays, pastel greens, and sometimes reds. In fact, I think that the colors introduced in the postwar period were also particularly significant for the

recovery of modalities not previously considered, as the black color of machines was really a non-color. Generally speaking, the colors used were of increasingly light, "delicate" hues. We must remember that eventually even filled and empty volumes were considered as colors, leading to an interpretation of contrasts that were also due to the shadows of empty spaces, grooving and engraving, which were all the more evident because they were set on the surfaces of bright, pure areas, such as those that were colored white or light gray.

There is also a connection here with Marcello Nizzoli, whose *Olivetti Lexikon 80* typewriter (1946/48) offered a bright beige-gray, or a particularly light and restful gray-green. The colors were generally adopted for the entire object, apart from a few specific features such as the keyboard. It was not until 1957, in the design for the *Mirella*, that Nizzoli tried to overcome the difficulty that came from "dissecting" the body into separate parts by conceiving them with dark and light colorings. Thus color also acquired the ingenious ability to emphasize the analytical reading of parts in industrial objects.

After various experiments, the Vespa was presented, standing out against the background of Italian roads with increasingly light colors, such as cream, light green, or gray, although some parts, such as the handlebars and headlight, retained a certain autonomy. There was the famous very pale metallic gray of the *150 GS* in 1955 (Max Meyer color number 15005), contrasting with the long, dark green seat, and the almost white gray of the *160 GS* in 1962 (Max Meyer 1.298.8714), combinations that gave exceptional elegance, also due to the chrome-plated trim in the second case.

Red requires a special mention. The precedents were Alfa Romeo (later imitated by Ferrari) and Moto Guzzi, that had adopted a particular red, a very Italian orangey red (I am convinced that "earthy" colors—such as sienna and cinnabar, with its intense hue—are very present in the minds of Italian designers and artists, and are innate in us). It may be noted that the vehicles in question were "aggressive." The *Vespa 180 SS* sports model produced in 1965 was offered in three shades of red, and also in hawthorn and peacock blue. It was the first vehicle with a license plate that was offered to the public in various colors, following the policy that began with the 50-cc model in 1964.

Social habits changed radically after the war. Large manufacturers in the north of Italy—in Turin, Milan, and Genoa—resumed activity and called for workers. The workers who moved to the factories were of peasant stock, but the experiences they had had were different from those of their parents. Many had been obliged, as soldiers, to leave their homes for long periods, traveling to very distant places, and they had seen new realities. They were all seeking ways of improving their own conditions with new determination.

As Andrea Branzi says:

"The Italy that emerged from the war that it had lost was a country that, precisely because of the defeat that it had suffered, was able to turn over a new page with regard to its embarrassing past, drawing advantage from a break with its most recent history. From the great physical destruction that it had undergone it could have set in motion a material reconstruction adapted to European models. That is not exactly how things happened ..."

(Andrea Branzi, *Introduzione al design italiano, una modernità incompleta*, Baldini&Castoldi, Milan, p. 104.)

The traditional form of transport had always been the train, but now it was time to change. With the progress of economic conditions and the increase in demands, now there was an attempt to offer a form of transport that would be economical in terms of basic price, consumption, and maintenance. It also had to be reasonably fast, suitable for traveling to work and making small journeys, and it had to be able to carry a passenger as well. At the weekend whole families could be seen setting off for simple outings, using the Vespa in unlikely ways.

The Vespa on roads and motorways

The Vespa: the vehicle that was a symbol of postwar reconstruction. In 1947, with what became known as the Marshall Plan, the United States sought to encourage the reconstruction of countries destroyed by the war, and at the same time draw them into its own political orbit. Piaggio was one of the companies that obtained a few thousand dollars to acquire presses, American of course, in order to improve its manufacture of Vespas.

In 1950 the Institute for Industrial Reconstruction created Autostrade Concessioni e

Costruzioni S.p.A. (Motorway Concessions and Construction), a company that—together with other large industrial groups—became one of the key players in the postwar reconstruction of Italy and the economic boom of the sixties.

In 1956 the first agreement between Autostrade and ANAS (Autonomous National Highway Company) was signed, for construction and operation of the main artery linking north and south in Italy, the "Motorway of the Sun" (A1 Milan–Naples).

The symbol of the Motorway of the Sun, and therefore of the reconstruction, was the church of St John the Baptist, associated with the renewal of the country and the plan for the reunification of Italy. The architect Giovanni Michelucci was commissioned to design the work in September 1960. By December of the same year the design for the church had been defined. The complex, built on the plain of the township of Campi Bisenzio to the west of Florence, alongside the ribbon of the motorway, has a volume that makes a powerful, intensely expressive visual impact, giving the impression to passersby of a tent for modern caravanserais.

Utility vehicles

The Italians in their automobiles began to travel along the motorway that linked north and south. The Fiat *Seicento* (designed by Dante Giacosa) was launched at the Geneva Motor Show in 1955—a utility vehicle with rear-mounted engine, independent four-wheel suspension, and bodywork with a self-supporting structure. Including the *Multipla* version, over 950,000 of these automobiles were manufactured up to 1960, a total that rises to 4,034,000 if vehicles produced under license are also included.

The *Nuova Cinquecento*, by the same designer, was presented in the summer of 1957. It had a rear-mounted, 2-cylinder, air-cooled engine. When production ceased in 1975, 3,678,000 units had been manufactured.

The gradual expansion of the motorway system was a contributing cause for the production of two models in 1961, with the same body but a larger engine, in two versions: the *Milletrecento* (1300 cc) and the *Millecinquecento* (1500 cc), inspired by American automobiles. Other models that were manufactured were the *1800 B*, the *2300*, the *2300 S coupé*, and new models of the *Millecento* (1100 cc).

It seemed then that the Vespa had reached a crisis and would be replaced by the automobile.

Nevertheless, the Vespa calmly continued to circulate, even on motorways.

PRODUCT TRADEMARK AND LOGO

Curiously, Vespa used two logos: one corresponding to Piaggio and one that we could define as corresponding specifically to Vespa.

At the beginning of the events we are describing, the Piaggio mark on the product was a simple, heraldic-style shield, with a capital "P" (Piaggio) in elegant Bodoni lettering, and it also bore the legend "Piaggio Genova." The shield was divided into two fields, and the "P" was in white on a light and dark blue background. This trademark was often used, although not always. Intermittently, the shield with the Piaggio "P" appeared engraved on the rubber sleeve of the handlebar grips, without the "Piaggio Genova" specification. Sometimes the name "Piaggio" appeared in full.

In the early sixties the "P" was combined with the "G" and took on a different style. The new trademark had, in fact, been the subject of a competition, but the company chose not to use the winning entry and instead adopted the trademark designed by Emilio De Silva, who enclosed it all in a hexagon, still against a background of the company blue.

The Vespa Logo

Here, however, we are interested in examining the Vespa logo, which we could consider as a special product identity. It looks like a signature produced by a pen. It is presented in a fluttering italic, continuous and underlined, with the capital strongly marked, emphasizing that it is an individual name.

The first letter curves impulsively forward, as if to inject speed into the name. Yet the "e" immediately after it seems to slope backward, as if to blend speed with prudence.

In some cases, such as the *Vespa 125* in 1958, the name "Vespa" is in relief and is

1951 - VESPA SILURO

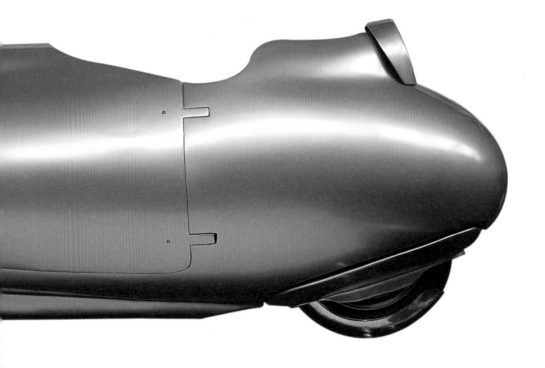

attached to the front shield by light aluminum rivets.

Sometimes further lettering, such as *GS*, or *Super Sport* (1964), was added to the Vespa logo, contained within the underlining. A large number of other names and letters appeared on the vehicle, on the sides, at the back, or inside the shield.

The British manufacturer Douglas, which made a certain number of Vespas under license in the early fifties, attached a Douglas "signature" in imitation of the lucky name of Vespa. Other variants were the *Vespa Hoffmann,* made north of Düsseldorf as a result of the 1949 agreement, and the *Vespa Allstate* in 1951, with its very American blazons, sold in the United States.

Company identity and special vehicles

If we consider the identity of a company as the sum of various actions connected with the world outside it, we must remember that the prime architect of the Piaggio company's identity was the product itself, followed by the immediate perception of the importance of Vespa Clubs, and therefore their promotion. And a far from unimportant boost was provided by its prominent presence in many very successful movies, some of which even helped to convey the special quality of the Italian lifestyle to other countries. The Vespa played a leading part in that style. However, the relationship between the Vespa and the movies is discussed in another section of this publication.

I would like to add that the Archive and the Museum are also the expression of a strong company identity. They contain the history of the company and its products. Nowadays the Archive continues to be a focus for careful studies and research, while a series of museum professionals have made their contribution on the exhibition side.

Among many interesting initiatives we can mention the construction of certain buildings, such as the Piaggio Mountain Colony in Santo Stefano D'Aveto and the Piaggio village in Pontedera.

The company did not fail to produce some special vehicles (for image purposes, one might say), such as the *Vespa Alpha* prepared for the film *Dick Smart 2007* (1967). In the fictitious world of the movie it could even fly, transforming itself into a helicopter, or submerge like a submarine.

1951 - VESPA 125 U

1951 - VESPA 125

1958 - VESPA 125

Some military vehicles were mass produced, especially in response to orders placed by the French army for the war in Indochina.

Two competition models of the Vespa were made in 1950: the first record was established on the Montlhéry racetrack, where the Vespa (with streamlined design for the occasion) reached a speed of 85 mph. The *Vespa Siluro* established a new record, achieving over 106 mph on the Rome-Ostia track.

EVOLUTION OF MODELS

1948-1951 – *Vespa 125*

In the version first produced in 1948 the body was load-bearing but reinforced. The engine cowl was open at the front to allow the fitting of a rear shock absorber coupled to a spring, thus correcting the serious initial defect of the *98*, which had the transverse engine resting on a rubber buffer (semi-rigid suspension) that often caused the frame to break. The front mudguard was made more slender to facilitate wheel-changing, a solution typical of the first three years of production. The handlebar design was also perfected, with two rubber grips bearing the Piaggio trademark.

A sidecar version was also studied. The overall height was 950 mm, the seat was set at 760 mm, and the footrest platform at 220 mm. The headlight had a characteristic 95-mm chrome-plated ring, subtly decorated with a small crest. This model was specifically aimed at tourism and sport.

The 1951 version of the *Vespa 125* was made famous by the movie *Roman Holiday*. In the early fifties, output had reached 6,000 units a month. In 1953 the *125 U* (utility version) was launched, together with a new series of the *Vespa 125*, with a refined, elegant design. The Vespa logo was reproduced directly on the front shield, painted on.

1955 – *150 GS*

Among the models made in the fifties the very attractive *Vespa 150 GS* (Gran Sport) stood out, recognized as the scooter with the most harmonious, elegant design in the world, the

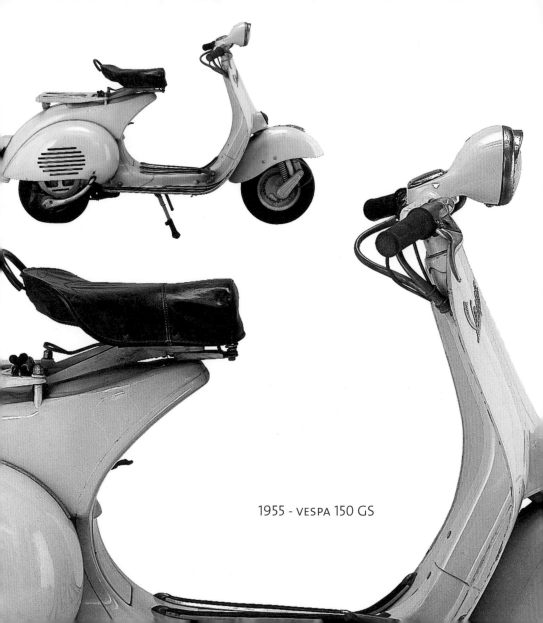

1955 - VESPA 150 GS

1955 - VESPA GS

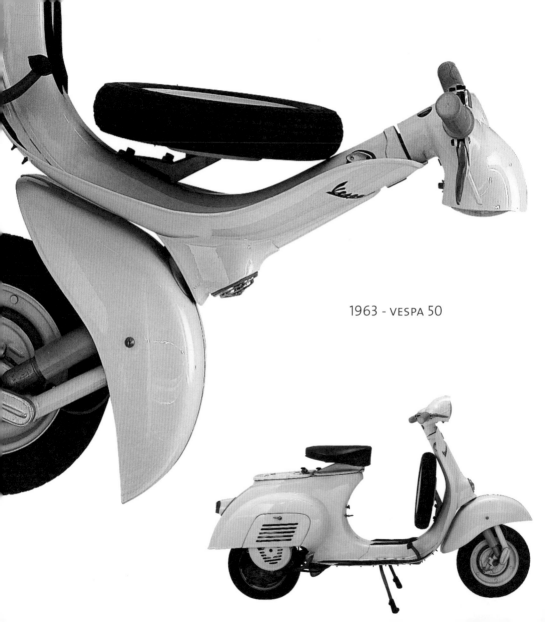

1963 - VESPA 50

model most appreciated, imitated, and remembered, according to many.

The *GS* has an evident sporting style, derived from the Piaggio racing team's experiences in competitions.

The appearance was characterized by a harmonious balance of different elements: the new die-cast handlebars, the 115-mm headlight with the milometer incorporated into it, and the shield, which was resized and curved, as if to enclose and protect the rider's legs. Above all there was the adoption of bright silver metallic paintwork, making the volumes look lighter. The dark green seat was extended to form a single unit, making it even more suitable for carrying two people or for the typical prostrate position of racing motorcyclists, and the two side cowls were also larger and higher because of the different placement of the carburetor. The result, apart from enhancing the appearance, also improved the aerodynamics. A characteristic shiny aluminum rounded edging was adopted on the side cowls and front mudguard that contained the large 10-inch wheels. The brightly shining kick-start pedal was longer than on previous models and was fitted with black non-slip rubber. The millionth Vespa was manufactured on April 28, 1956.

Many new models appeared between 1958 and the beginning of the sixties, such as the *Vespa 125* (1958), with a central steering column and handlebars with totally inbuilt controls and central welding between the two half-bodies of the frame, at the rear of the cowl. This model was followed in 1960 by the *Vespa 150* and another version of the *Vespa 125*. As of 1958 the headlight no longer appeared on the front mudguard.

1962 – *Vespa 125* and *Vespa 160 GS*

The year 1962 was characterized by production of the very powerful *Vespa 160 GS*, with a second, luxury series made ready in 1963. This second model was distinguished by the remarkable care shown in the design, with the spare wheel contained in the left compartment and storage space arranged behind the windshield, still with the characteristic profile. In the meantime the silvery color of the first *GS* had become white, described as white lead gray or pale gray. The body also looked light and agile because of the system of central welding. As a result the mudguard seemed to consist of two half-shells, strengthened internally along the connection and ornamented with a small shiny aluminum crest.

1972 - VESPA 200 RALLY

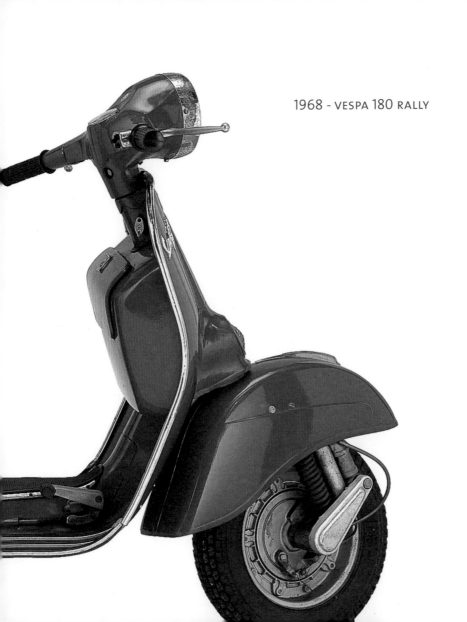

1968 - VESPA 180 RALLY

1963 – *Vespa 150 GL* and *Vespa 50*

The *Vespa 150 GL*, considered the most elegant design that the Piaggio engineers have produced, appeared in 1963. Also noteworthy was the first version of the *Vespa 50*, the legendary "Vespino" that became the dream of generations of youngsters. It was a single-seater, weighed only 145 pounds, had three gears, and looked agile and well-balanced, with the side bulges raised, pressed as a single piece with the body, stress-bearing as usual. The length was 1630 mm and the width was 610 mm.

This model also marked the beginning of a more organized color policy, including metallic coloring, although color variations were produced to order, as was the long seat.

In the mid-sixties Piaggio ushered in the moped era: *Ciao*, *Bravo*, and *Sì* were some of the models in this light, elegant line aimed at young riders.

Then came the *Vespa 180 SS* (1964), and the *Vespa Nuova 125* and *Vespa 90 Super Sport* (both in 1966).

The development and perfecting of models continued in the late sixties and the seventies. Some of the names to remember are the *Vespa 125 Primavera* and *Vespa Rally 180* (1968), *Vespa 50 Elestart* (1970), *Vespa Rally 200* (1972), *Vespa 50S* (1973), and *Vespa 125 ET3* (1976), with the new Piaggio trademark and Vespa name.

DESIGN AND SYSTEMS

In the late sixties and early seventies, markets were increasingly dominated by a commercial race to produce increasingly complex objects more and more quickly, also because of the introduction of electronic components, favoring faster development of models.

Design switched its field of exploration and planning from the single product to a group of interrelated objects, and then went on to analyze the practice of designing for groups of items. This type of design was known as "process for systems." In this way designers successfully sought to study whole families of products, with a technical elaboration that could be adapted to market developments.

A well-known example of this new design process was the Swedish Hasselblad company.

1973 - VESPA 50 SPECIAL

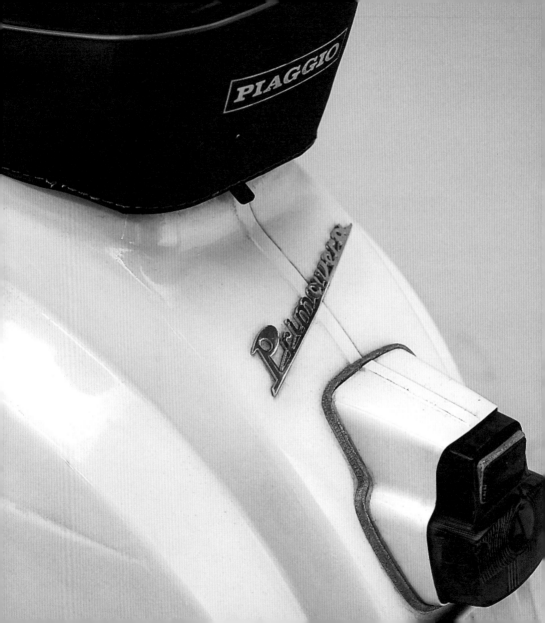

1968 - VESPA 125 PRIMAVERA

1976 - VESPA 125 ET3 PRIMAVERA

1978 - VESPA P125X

Hasselblad had started in 1940, supplying photographic equipment (*Ross HK7*) to the Swedish Air Force. Then, in 1948, Victor Hasselblad put his first "Hasselblad" on sale.

It was the first modular camera, with a central body to which it was possible to attach a variety of screw-mount lenses, interchangeable film backs, and viewing systems. Some years later, everyone admired and studied the splendid *Hasselblad 500 C/M*, produced from 1970 to 1989. The cubical central body contained the interchangeable lens and viewfinder—exchangeable with pentaprisms and other accessories—while the film magazine on the back was removable and could also be changed with the film partially exposed. The central *Syncro Compur* shutter was integrated with the lenses: the standard lens was a *Zeiss Planar T 80 mm f/2.8*, also interchangeable.

On a distant July 20 in 1969 we felt the excitement of hearing the cry "Touchdown! Touchdown!" when the American Apollo 11 mission landed on the Moon. The expedition used the *HDC* (*Hasselblad Data Camera*), nicknamed the *Moon Camera.*

The more attentive designers understood the possibilities that it offered and set out to overcome the difficulties connected with rapid development of products by starting to design for systems.

Then there were Ettore Sottsass's designs for work systems and Mario Bellini's designs for calculators, both for Olivetti.

The result was that first of all designers defined families of products that were linked in terms of form, suitable for subsequent completion by various different technologies, corresponding to different features and functions. In fact, there was an idea of proposing general guidelines to be observed. As a result, it became increasingly important to examine the logical and analytical composition of products so as to be able to design the components separately.

Piaggio also opted for this direction with the *PX* line.

1978 – *Vespa PX*

Designed in the late seventies, this model represents an ideal continuation between the very first models and the present ones. This Vespa remains faithful to the traditional stress-bearing pressed metal body with a raised mudguard. The bulkier appearance makes it roomier, and the front shock absorber has become hydraulic. The saddle is made of expanded polyurethane, in line with the development of soft materials used by designers for upholstery.

Over two million *Vespa PX* scooters have been produced and it has now become a symbol of Italian design and style, still sold in the traditional engine sizes: 125, 150, and 200. The *Vespa P125X* (1978) is still in production after 24 years, as is the *Vespa P200X*. Also noteworthy are the *Vespa PK* (1983) and the *Vespa ET4 Gran Turismo* (1996–2003).

Vespa PX Red

Among the other models produced during those years we could mention the *Vespa PX 150* (1981), *Vespa PX 200*, and *Vespa PX 150 E* (1982), *Vespa PK 125* and *Vespa PK 50* (1983), *Vespa PK 125 A* (1984), *Vespa PK 50 A, Vespa P125 ETS*, and *Vespa T5 Pole Position* (1985), *Cosa* and *Cosa 2* (1988), and the *Vespa N* (1989).

The *Sfera* was presented in 1991, with a 50-cc engine and plastic body, which was an anomaly for Piaggio. That year the *Sfera* won the "Compasso d'Oro" Prize and, with sales of 58,000, was the most sold scooter in Europe at the time. That year also saw the launching of the *Vespa 50* special revival. In 1994 there was the *Vespa T5*, and in 1996 the *ET4 125*.

The story is still continuing with the success of the new generation of Vespas, begun in 1996 to mark the fiftieth anniversary, including the four-stroke *Vespa ET4 125*, always at the top of European sales figures, the *Vespa ET4 150*, and the latest addition to the fold, the 50-cc *Vespa ET4*.

From the original Vespa in 1946 to the *Beverly* in 2001, over a hundred different scooter models have been designed and introduced.

1952 - VESPA 6 GIORNI

1965 - VESPA 90SS

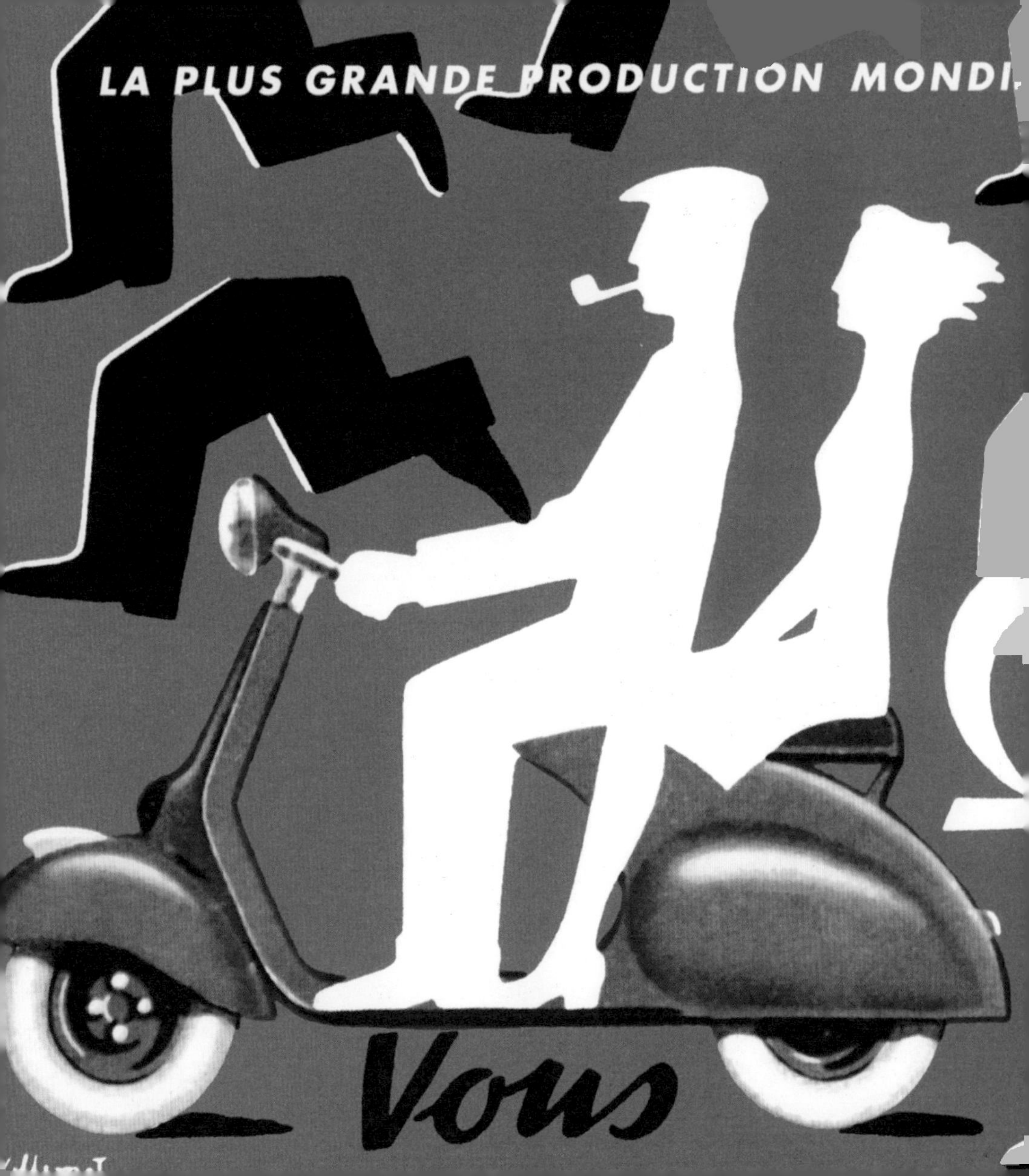
LA PLUS GRANDE PRODUCTION MONDI
Vous

Oggi sono

PERCHÉ...

Gaia Milani

APPLES AND WINGS

In 1949, three years after production of the first *Vespa 98* began and one year after the first *125*, the hum of forty thousand vehicles circulating on the roads drew a faint question mark in the blue sky on a leaflet that bore the title "Why is the Vespa 125 the most widely used in the world?"

Apart from the various models and answers that were given, Piaggio succeeded in its bid to find a solution to the urgent need for recovery, productivity, mobility, and relaxation at a time when people were beginning to glimpse the end of the war.

Like a bold and joyful cry, "*Vespizzatevi*" ("Vespify!"), with its faintly military echo, was the imperative that continued to appear on Ferenzi's posters until the mid-fifties. Set against a background of flat colors, slender, busy figures issued their invitation: get moving, travel around, meet up, work, get back your energy and your confidence.

By 1956 a million Vespas had been produced and the years spent astride this industrious object were revealing its ability to become a "Paradise for two." In 1961 the slogan was softened to "The only thing their happiness lacks is a Vespa," but the decision to switch attention from the object to its ability to influence behavior was reaffirmed. Two figures sitting on empty space. As in other campaigns, where the Vespa was little more than a silhouette, the objective was to establish the name, which became a synonym for scooter in ordinary language, and to associate it with values such as happiness and lightheartedness, and with the freedom given by the possibilities that the motorization of the individual opened up.

In the mid-sixties there was a decisive change of target. The standard market became the young user, to whom the production of the *Vespa 50* was devoted. Legally it could be ridden from the age of 14, without a vehicle license plate or a driving license. The Vespa became a pet produced in cheerful reds and yellows. A rainbow of ice white, moonbeam gray, amethyst gray, apple green, turquoise, light blue, Chinese blue, aquamarine blue, orange, purple, and even shocking pink, which in the early seventies began to appear transformed into an apple-shaped tongue-twister.

"*Chi Vespa mangia le mele. Chi non Vespa, no.*" "If you Vespa you eat the apples. If you don't Vespa, you go without." Just that. Under the artistic direction of Gilberto Filippetti there was an explosion of humorous, nonconformist public relations that captured the cheeky vitality of a generation of bold twenty-year-olds in search of hippy flowers and pop fields. Every apple was there to be picked: an outing, a story, a kiss. A juicy comic strip balloon in which to write a wish.

In 1972 war was declared on the "sardine-mobiles." Automobiles, transformed into flocks of psychedelic fish, were contrasted with a vocabulary consisting of words like respect, peace, and breathing space. "Sardine-mobiles don't get the fun of the sun. It's the Vespa rider that radiates." City scenes were replaced by sun, meadows, and beaches in a new search for areas of the countryside to be savored, yet the real message was that it did not matter who you were with or where, on your own or in groups, as long as your hair was blowing in the wind. On a Vespa.

In the eighties the Vespa also remembered its airplane heart, in a campaign in Piaggio blue colors that emphasized its presence in everyday life, design history, and the tradition of industrial production. The language moved ever closer to a world of imagery bound up with films and fashion, and even to a period nostalgia in the nineties, but at the heart of the message there was a sense of pride in the substantial continuity of forms and materials. In 2000 the "steel shutter" regained the sky-blue Piaggio shield that bore the name of Genoa, where the aeronautical plant was based.

"*The apple is a red heart with a green leaf / people eat it on their own or in groups, but always with their hair blowing in the wind / The ripe apple is eaten with the setting sun / the blue apple is eaten on the rocks / the starry apple is eaten with headlights shining …*" So: Vespa Pa Pa Pa.

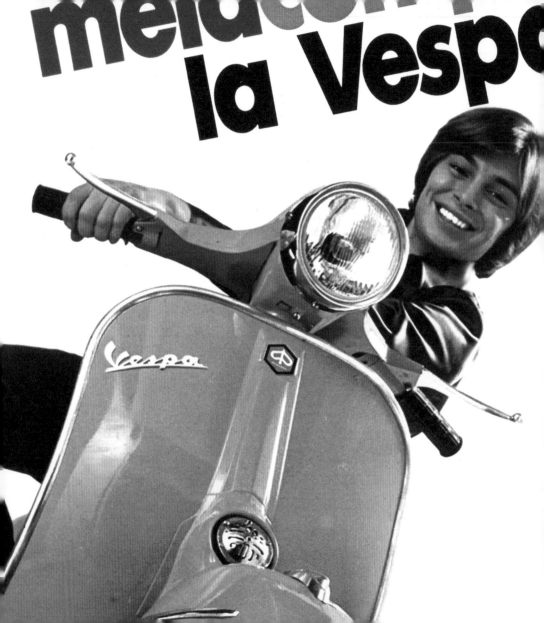

Mirco Melanco

THE VESPA IN THE MOVIES

The Vespa is the center of attention in movies in which the person that rides on it or owns it experiences feelings of love or friendship, moments of success, and the achievement of important goals, or, on the other hand, financial or psychological difficulties, or ideological clashes. The cinema is a fundamental promotional instrument for publicizing an industrial product among the masses. The Piaggio organization proved to be extremely skillful in this marketing operation, and its scooter became a symbol of modernity thanks to its constant appearances on the cinema screen.

Let's begin this brief analysis that weds the Vespa and the movies with three film titles well known to international audiences: *Roman Holiday*, *Quadrophenia*, and *Caro Diario*.

In William Wyler's movie *Roman Holiday*, the princess, Audrey Hepburn, and the reporter, Gregory Peck, experience magic feelings as they ride around on a Vespa, exploring a Rome resplendent with the beauty of magnificent monuments (the Colosseum, l'Altare della Patria, Via Condotti, and so on) and the fascination exercised by a city that in 1953 was animated by a period of fruitful rebirth. Hepburn and Peck were only the first in a long series of international actors that over the years have been portrayed riding on the most famous scooter in the world, in films that include Gene Kelly's *The Happy Road* (1957), Jacques Poitrenaud's *The Door Slams* (1960) with Catherine Deneuve, George Lucas's *American Graffiti* (1973), Julien Temple's *Absolute Beginners* (1986) with David Bowie, Betty Kaplan's *Of Love and Shadows* (1994) with Antonio Banderas, Paul Weitz's *American Pie* (1999), Anthony Minghella's *The Talented Mr. Ripley* (1999), Kevin Lima's *102 Dalmatians* (2000), and Charles Shyer's recent *Alfie* (2004). After the traumas of the Second World War, the Hollywood Vespa seen in *Roman Holiday* was an intelligent response on the part of Italian industry as it sought to enter international markets, receiving a boost for this reawakening from economic aid provided by the Marshall Plan and drawn towards fashions and lifestyles that came from overseas. *Quadrophenia*, a British-produced musical movie by Franc Roddam (1979), inspired by The Who's record album and decisive for the singer Sting's film debut (in the part of Ace Face), showed England in the sixties as it looked on at the excursions of the Mods, groups of turbulent youngsters who were accustomed to narcotics and had elaborately equipped Vespas and Lambrettas. The Mods were constantly clashing with the Rockers, who rode powerful motorbikes and were very violent. Jimmy (Phil Daniels), the central character in the movie, steals a marvelous Vespa festooned with headlights of various sizes and colors, yet not much light falls on his own existence. Betrayed by the legal system and his friends and family, he flings himself over the cliffs of Dover. A clearly directorial decision shows us only the fall of the vehicle, while the young man's body is not seen. The final image in the movie shows the Vespa smashing on the rocks. In the first segment of *Caro Diario* (Dear Diary, 1994), entitled "On My Vespa," Nanni Moretti travels around in a sleepy, deserted Rome on a sunny summer's day. He rides his blue two-wheeler as if he were gliding over a snowy slope, exploring the districts of Garbatella, Casalpalocco, and Spinaceto. Moretti expresses his sensations as a traveler with regard to the architecture of the city and the nature of its inhabitants, and he recounts his ideas about an intense, intimate, personalized Rome. The director continues on his journey until he comes to Ostia, to the place where Pier Paolo Pasolini died. Three very different movies, but three stories that are out of the ordinary, assigning very different destinies to a form of locomotion capable of conveying very special sensations as it constantly explores new places and landscapes, like the new feelings of its riders who reveal their individual sensibility in relation to life's issues. The Vespa helps to overcome geographical spaces, but also, and especially, mental spaces, apparently able to govern emotional actions and reactions.

In the movie *Totò Looks for an Apartment* by Mario Monicelli and Steno (1949), the Vespa is the "wish" that does not appear on the screen but is talked about in the kitchen. Totò's daughter cannot afford to buy one, but she hopes to win the scooter in a competition organized by Sarti Soda. She tells her father. The great Neapolitan actor plays semantically with the ambiguity between the meanings of *vespa* (wasp) and Vespa (scooter):

"A wasp? What wasp? Where's the wasp?"

"No, Dad, it's the name of the vehicle you win."

"Ah, the Vespa!"

For Italians in the fifties and sixties, riding on the saddle of a Vespa meant, above all, doing so in company, or else roaming around by the sea (*Sunday in August*, 1950), or performing veritable feats, as in *A Day in Court*. Some youngsters from Gardone Val Trompia, in the province of Brescia, belong to an association of Vespa and Lambretta owners. They travel over 370 miles to see the Pope. Getting to Rome turns out to be no great problem for them, according to the priest (Walter Chiara) that leads the reckless band: "Yes, because when the goal is pleasing, you don't feel the exertion. And as the miles went by, instead of feeling tired we felt happy. We sang and sang ..."

The song *Per amor del motore* is sung by some Teddy boys, Vespa owners off to the pine forests of Appia Antica in search of solitude. In this movie (*Howlers of the Dock*, 1960) Adriano Celentano rides a comfortable Vespa with a sidecar. In *Female Three Times* (1959) the final sequences of the film look like an advertisement for the Vespa: young Italians scooting around on the outskirts of Rome with beautiful Russian gymnasts riding pillion behind them, happy to go off with their lovers after being freed from the rigid control of the Soviet agents. Paolo (Umberto Orsini) takes Marcella (Mina) home on his Vespa and all his Vespa-riding friends follow behind them, traveling first through the center of Rome and then through the outskirts, where the expansion of the city is getting out of hand, with the construction of enormous, anonymous housing projects (*Io bacio... tu baci*, 1961). In *La dolce vita* (1960) the reporters rush off to get their scoop, whizzing across the capital on their speedy Vespas. And in *Madri pericolose* (1960) there's also a reporter that pursues his prey on a Piaggio scooter. In the opening sequences of *Fist in His Pocket* (1965) two rash youngsters end up on the ground when their Vespa skids on the gravel. In *Friends for Life* (1955) Mario, a ten-year-old boy, learns to ride a Vespa and in the same movie, during a Vespa rally, another boy says: "If you went in for Vespas, you'd be a champion."

The Vespa is also the right vehicle for scoring with girls by riding together in a harmonious group, forming a swarm of "wasps" (*Poor But Beautiful*, 1957). A man that works as a fireman (Raf Vallone) follows the beautiful Agnese (Sophia Loren) and eventually finds a suitable excuse to get her to ride on the saddle of his scooter, a Vespa with a windshield, and he takes her to an interview for a job in an elegant office in the center of Rome (*The Sign of Venus*, 1955). A young man is happy to own a scooter on which he can finally take his girlfriend out for rides, getting away from his own district and exploring the countryside, traveling along narrow, solitary, romantic roads (*A Tailor's Maid*, 1957). Lia (Antonella Lualdi), a chemist's daughter in a small town in the hills of Albano, uses her silver-colored Vespa skillfully to go down the valley and collect medical supplies (*Cani e gatti*, 1952). Two men in a smart convertible, with the typical appearance of 1960s "Latin lovers," observe two pretty girls roaming around on the roads of the Côte d'Azur on an elegant red Vespa (*Beach Casanova*, 1962). An American Italian (Walter Chiari), repatriated to Ravenna, prefers to park his Cadillac and travel around town on an easy-to-ride Vespa that makes him feel more Italian (*A Bride for Frank*, 1956). Aroldo follows his girlfriend Delia (Delia Scala) from Rome to Milan on a Vespa, coming up against all kinds of difficulties, but he is able to move around freely because he is unaffected by the rail and bus strikes called for those dates (*Bellezze in bicicletta*, 1950). On the roads of Ischia the characteristic open carriages have undergone a metamorphosis: drawn by a Vespa instead of a horse or donkey, they have comfortable seats and a colorful sunshade (*Holiday Island*, 1958), beneath which even Charlie Chaplin and his wife went for a ride, as the pictures of an INCOM Week newsreel show. In the fifties and sixties many newsreels showed the Vespa as a vehicle that symbolized the progress of Italian industry. They were pictures shot directly in the factory, or on test circuits where expert riders performed daring acrobatics, or else on the road in Italy or elsewhere, as in a spectacular scene of scooters passing beneath the Arc de Triomphe in Paris. In another newsreel, a nice gag shows the leading actors Alberto Sordi and Aldo Fabrizi during a pause on a film set: Sordi pretends to brake and make his companion tumble off, but when Fabrizi is seen still sitting on the rear seat he whizzes away, leaving him standing. In those years, reports from foreign correspondents described Italy as "the land of the Vespa," and the part played by the Piaggio scooter in international customs is documented by its presence in many movies, though it is often difficult to see because the directors showed it

in very quick shots, as in Michelangelo Antonioni's *L'Avventura*, in the final sequence of Federico Fellini's *Nights of Cabiria*, in Mario Monicelli's "Renzo and Luciana" segment in *Boccaccio '70*, and in Alfred Hitchcock's *To Catch a Thief.*

Marcello Mastroianni carries two friends on the saddle of a Vespa with a windshield, while the scenery behind them is the outskirts of Rome at the height of the building expansion (*My Wife's Enemy*, 1959). And a polygamist (Ugo Tognazzi) uses a Vespa to escape from his two wives (*Menage Italian Style*, 1965).

A rather hoity-toity girl has to put up with traveling around the Riviera Ligure on a Vespa that belongs to a swimming-pool attendant (*Love on the Riviera*, 1958):

"Did you bring the Cadillac?"

"No, I have the Vespa!"

For these short journeys by the sea the Vespa is certainly ideal. But are we laying too much stress on rebellious youngsters?

Another girl, in contrast, wants to ride a motor scooter on the busy streets of the city or on the quieter roads of the outskirts and invites a boy to take a seat as a passenger (*First Love*, 1958):

"Get on behind, take my bag, and don't hold on to me too tightly because I'm ticklish."

Maria is a young girl in Florence who refuses to get on because the Vespa seems to have lost its magical persuasive power of love over her (*Porta un bacione a Firenze*, 1956):

"I want to take you for a ride on the Vespa."

"On that contraption?"

"You used to come once."

"I was younger once."

The Vespa and Vespa riders are generally viewed with approval. However, a notary (Aroldo Tieri) in Avellara, a small town in Lazio, who is a staunch defender of public morality, considers scooter riders rather unsavory specimens (*È permesso, maresciallo?* aka *Tuppe tuppe, marescià!*, 1958):

"Look at those motor scooters [*turning as a Vespa goes by with a boy and a girl on it*]. Instruments of perdition!"

The years go by and the Vespa continues to appear in Italian movies, although the competition has intensified year by year—in the fifties and sixties the only challenger was the Lambretta, which was featured in numerous films, among which I recall *Come September* (1961) with Gina Lollobrigida and Rock Hudson, often mistakenly included in filmographies devoted to the Vespa—with numerous models of scooters manufactured by Italian, French, Japanese, and Korean companies. As one follows the Vespa's journeys one realizes that things are gradually changing: the scenery in the city and outside it alters, and also the behavior and language of Vespa owners. In Sicily, in the early seventies, Rosalia gets a job in a "super-swift laundry chain." She describes her important achievement in a letter to her husband, also a worker, who has moved to Turin, while the screen shows pictures of her riding a yellow *Vespa 50* with images of the Madonna and other saints drawn on the windshield (*The Seduction of Mimi*, 1972):

"(…) and paying great attention to moral and material considerations [*she fastens her skirt with a clip to stop the wind raising it as she rides along*], Ielenuzza taught me how to handle a motorcycle and now I've become a skilled rider and, if you let me, with time I'm thinking of buying it by installments."

Carlo Vanzina is the Italian director who has used the Vespa most frequently in his Italian-style comedies, such as *Time for Loving* (1983), *My First Forty Years* (1987), and *Il cielo in una stanza* (1999): the motorcycle idealizes the dimensions of a romanticism that belongs to the past, the nostalgia for a time that, alas, can never return. *Il Grande Blek* (1987) also relives stories and passions of the early sixties, offering, among other things, an exciting impromptu race between a Vespa and a Lambretta. Agostina Belli accompanies a man on a Vespa to the place where the body of his wife is discovered (*Double Murder*, 1978). In *Forever Mary* (1989) and *Boys on the Outside* (1990) Marco Risi describes the limits of an increasingly violent society in decline, especially for youngsters that belong to the most deprived social classes, like the ones that end up in the Malaspina juvenile prison in Palermo. These youngsters use the Vespa to ride to a house where a prostitute is waiting for them, to escape from the police that are chasing them, or to smash an automobile window with the spark plug. In *Damned the Day I Met You* (1992) Carlo Verdone uses the Vespa to speed away from the psychoanalyst, and in the same film Margherita Buy rides the scooter with Verdone behind her, heavily laden with bags of shopping. Gerry Calà is *Il*

ragazzo del Pony Express (1986), using his white Vespino with great skill and performing impromptu acrobatics in the streets of Milan before the astonished eyes of his friends. Paolo Rossi in *Kamikazen – Ultima notte a Milano* (1987) and Stefano Accorsi in *Jack Frusciante è uscito dal gruppo* (1996) play the part of restless youths who enact their stories dashing about on Vespas, but the solution to their worries still seems very far away. In the countryside on the outskirts of Naples, Iaia Forte plays the part of a prostitute: she has a faithful friend who likes to watch her as he "works" lying on a Vespino (*Black Holes*, 1995). The scene is very different in Lampedusa, in *Respiro: Grazia's Island*, a film by Emanuele Crialese (2002), where Pasquale shows off all sorts of acrobatics in the streets on his specially adapted Vespa, which is also used to ride as a threesome. The Vespa is the central focus of the film. It is the trusty vehicle that knows all the boy's secrets, including the hiding of his mother (Valeria Golino) in a cave to avoid a loathed journey to Milan, a removal that the townspeople want because they are disturbed by the carefree attitude and freedom with which she lives.

102 Dalmatians by Kevin Lima (2000)

Absolute Beginners by Julien Temple (1986)

Adorable and a Liar by Nunzio Malasomma (1958)

Against the Law by Flavio Calzavara (1950)

Alfie by Charles Shyer (2004)

Always on Sunday by Giulio Petroni (1962)

American Graffiti by George Lucas (1973)

American in Paris, An by Vincente Minnelli (1951)

American in Rome, An [Audio only] by Steno (1954)

American Pie by Paul Weitz (1999)

Austin Powers – International Man of Mystery by Jay Roach (1997)

Avventura, L' by Michelangelo Antonioni (1960)

Bad Girls Don't Cry by Mauro Bolognini (1959)

Beach Casanova by Vittorio Sala (1962)

Bellezze in bicicletta by Carlo Campogalliani (1950)

Bidone, Il by Federico Fellini (1955)

Black Holes by Pappi Corsicato (1995)

Boccaccio '70 (Act IV: "Renzo and Luciana")
    by Mario Monicelli (1962)

Bombers B-52 by Gordon Douglas (1957)

Boy and a Girl, A by Marco Risi (1984)

Boys on the Outside by Marco Risi (1990)

Bread, Love and Dreams by Luigi Comencini (1953)

Bride for Frank, A by Leonardo De Mitri (1956)

Cani e gatti by Leonardo De Mitri (1952)

Caro Diario (first segment: "On My Vespa") by Nanni Moretti (1994)

Cheaters, The by Marcel Carné (1958)

Ciao ciao bambina by Sergio Grieco (1959)

Cielo in una stanza, Il by Carlo Vanzina (1999)

Conversation, The by Francis Ford Coppola (1974)

Damned the Day I Met You by Carlo Verdone (1992)

Day in Court, A by Steno (1954)

Defeated Victor, The by Paolo Heusch (1958)

Dick Smart 2007 by Frank Shannon (Franco Prosperi) (1967)

Dolce vita, La by Federico Fellini (1960)

Door Slams, The by Jacques Poitrenaud (1960)

Double Murder by Steno (1978)

Dreams in a Drawer by Renato Castellani (1957)

È permesso, maresciallo? by Carlo Ludovico Bragaglia (1958)

Eighteen in the Sun by Camillo Mastrocinque (1962)

European Nights by Alessandro Blasetti (1959)

Fast and Sexy by Carlo Lastricati (1958)

Female Three Times by Steno (1959)

First Love by Mario Camerini (1958)

Fist in His Pocket by Marco Bellocchio (1966)

For the First Time by Rudolph Maté (1959)

Forever Mary by Marco Risi (1989)

Friends for Life by Franco Rossi (1955)

Getting Away with It the Italian Way by Lucio Fulci (1962)

Girl of San Pietro Square, The by Piero Costa (1958)

Grande Blek, Il by Giuseppe Piccioni (1987)

Happy Road, The by Gene Kelly (1957)

Hit and Run by Bernard Borderie (1959)

Holiday Island by Mario Camerini (1958)

Howlers of the Dock by Lucio Fulci (1960)

Io bacio… tu baci by Piero Vivarelli (1961)

Jack Frusciante è uscito dal gruppo by Enza Negroni (1996)

Jessica by Jean Negulesco and Oreste Palella (1962)

Kamikazen – Ultima notte a Milano by Gabriele Salvatores (1987)

Ladro lui, ladra lei by Luigi Zampa (1958)

Love and Larceny by Dino Risi (1960)

Love and Troubles [Audio only] by Angelo Dorigo (1958)

Love on the Riviera by Gianni Franciolini (1958)

Lucky Five, The by Mario Mattoli (1952)

Madri pericolose by Domenico Paolella (1960)

Mamma's Boy by Mauro Morassi (1957)

Man of Straw, A by Pietro Germi (1957)

Menage Italian Style by Franco Indovina (1965)

My First Forty Years by Carlo Vanzina (1987)

My Wife's Enemy by Gianni Puccini (1959)

New Angels, The by Ugo Gregoretti (1962)

Nights of Cabiria by Federico Fellini (1957)

No, My Darling Daughter by Ralph Thomas (1961)

Of Love and Shadows by Betty Kaplan (1994)

Overtaxed, The by Steno (1959)

Pair of Briefs, A by Ralph Thomas (1962)

Poor But Beautiful by Dino Risi (1957)

Poor Girl, Pretty Girl by Dino Risi (1957)

Porta un bacione a Firenze by Camillo Mastrocinque (1956)

Principe Fusto, Il by Maurizio Arena (1960)

Professor Nachtfalter by Rolf Meyer (1951)

Quadrophenia by Franc Roddam (1979)

Quanto sei bella Roma by Marino Girolami (1960)

Ragazzo del Pony Express, Il by Franco Amurri (1986)

Red Wood Pigeon by Nanni Moretti (1989)

Respiro: Grazia's Island by Emanuele Crialese (2002)

Roman Holiday by William Wyler (1953)

Rome Adventure by Delmer Daves (1962)

Seduction of Mimi, The by Lina Wertmüller (1972)

Sette chili in sette giorni by Luca Verdone (1986)

Sign of Venus, The by Dino Risi (1955)

Simpatico mascalzone by Mario Amendola (1959)

Sunday in August by Luciano Emmer (1950)

Sunday Is Always Sunday by Camillo Mastrocinque (1958)

Tailor's Maid, A by Mario Monicelli (1957)

Talented Mr. Ripley, The by Anthony Minghella (1999)

Time for Loving by Carlo Vanzina (1983)

To Catch a Thief by Alfred Hitchcock (1955)

Too Bad She's Bad by Alessandro Blasetti (1954)

Totò Looks for an Apartment [Audio only] by Steno and Mario Monicelli (1949)

Totò, Peppino and La Dolce Vita by Sergio Corbucci (1961)

World by Night by Luigi Vanzi (1959)

World of Suzie Wong, The by Richard Quine (1960)

BIBLIOGRAPHY

Brief bibliography for design

Germano Celant, *Marcello Nizzoli*, Comunità, Milan, 1968

Paolo Fossati, *Il design in Italia*, Einaudi, Turin, 1972

Pier Paride Vidari, texts for the book: *Design Process, Olivetti 1908/1978*, Olivetti, Milan

Pier Paride Vidari, *The Late Great Tradition of Corporate Design*, and *The Imposing Presence of Radio Televisione Italiana*, Print, New York, 1994

Andrea Branzi, Michele De Lucchi (eds.), *Il design italiano degli anni '50*, Editoriale Domus, Milan, 1980, p. 280 ff.

Vittorio Gregotti (ed.) et al., *Il disegno del prodotto industriale, Italia 1960-1980*, Electa, Milan, 1982, p. 271

Andrea Branzi, *Introduzione al design Italiano, una modernità incompleta*, Baldini&Castoldi, Milan, 1999, p. 104

Claudia Neumann, *Design in Italia*, Howard Buch Produktion, Bonn, 1999, and Rizzoli, Milan, 1999, p. 59

Charlotte & Peter Fiell, *Industrial Design A-Z*, Taschen, Cologne, 2000, Italian edition, p. 241

Silvana Annicchiarico, *1945-2000, Il design in Italia, 100 oggetti della Collezione Permanente del Design Italiano della Triennale di Milano*, Gangemi, Rome, 2001

Pier Paride Vidari, Mario Bellini, in: *Maestri Design italiano. Collezione Permanente Triennale di Milano* (catalogue edited by Silvana Annichiarico), Snoeck Editore, 2003

Essential bibliography for the history of the *Vespa*

Luigi Rivola, *Chi Vespa mangia le mele*, Giorgio Nada, 1993

Roberto Leardi, *Scooters italiani degli anni '40/'60*, Polo Books, Rome, 1998

Roberto Leardi, *Vespa – Storia di una leggenda*, Polo Books, Rome, 1999

Luigi Frisinghelli, Roberto Leardi, Giorgio Notari, *Vespa tecnica 1 – 1946-55*, CLD, Pontedera, 1998

Luigi Frisinghelli, Roberto Leardi, Giorgio Notari, *Vespa tecnica 2 – 1956-64*, CLD, Fornacette, 1999

Roberto Leardi, *Cinquant'anni di Vespa Club d'Italia 1949-1999*, CLD, Fornacette, 1999

Eric Brockway, S. Biancalana, *Vespa: An Illustrated History*, Giorgio Nada, 1999

Luigi Frisinghelli, Roberto Leardi, Giorgio Notari, *Vespa tecnica 3 – 1965-76*, CLD, Fornacette, 2000

Luigi Frisinghelli, Roberto Leardi, Giorgio Notari, *Vespa tecnica 4 – Record and Special Production*, CLD, Fornacette, 2001

Tommaso Fanfani, *Una leggenda verso i futuro, la storia della Piaggio*, Piaggio & C. S.p.A. and Fondazione Piaggio, Pisa, 2001

Omar Calabrese, Tommaso Fanfani (ed.), *Chi Vespa è... già domani. 56 anni di comunicazione Vespa*, Compositori Ed., 2002

Stefano Biancalana, Michele Marchianò, *La Vespa e tutti i suoi vespini*, Vimodrone, Giorgio Nada

Cinquanta anni di Vespa, Alinari IDEA, 2003

Davide Mazzanti, Ornella Sessa et al., *Vespa. Un'avventura italiana nel mondo*, Editore, Florence, 2003

Davide Mazzanti, Elissa Stein, *Vespa*, Chronicle Books, 2004

About Corradino D'Ascanio

Alberto Bassi, Marco Mulazzani, *Le macchine volanti di Corradino D'Ascanio*, Spazio Giorgetti di Milano, Electa-Giorgetti S.p.A., Milan, 1999–2000

Alberto Mondini, *Un'elica e due ruote: la libertà di muoversi – Vita di Corradino D'Ascanio*, Nistra-Lischi, Pisa, 1995

Magazines

Title	Number	Subject
Auto d'epoca	Jan. 2000	*History of the Vespa Rally 180 and 200*
Legend Bike	30 (Dec. 1994, p. 16)	*The 150 GS (1955)*
Legend Bike	41 and 84	*The 98*
Legend Bike	58	*The 125*
Legend Bike	68	*The 50 N*
Legend Bike	75	*The 90 Super Sprint*
Legend Bike	87 (Dec. 1999)	*The 150 (1956)*
Legend Bike	100 (Jan. 2001)	*The 180 Rally*
Legend Bike	128 (May 2003, p. 24)	*The Vespa Sport and Sei Giorni*
Moto storiche & d'epoca	Sept. 1997	*The Vespa TAP 56, made for the French paratroopers*
Moto storiche & d'epoca	Nov. 1997	*The Vespa made in Germany by Hoffmann*
Moto storiche & d'epoca	Nov. 1999	*The 150 GS type VS 5T*
Moto storiche & d'epoca	July 2000	*The 50 type V5 A1T*
Moto storiche & d'epoca	Dec. 2000 / Jan. 2001	*The 125 Primavera*
Moto storiche & d'epoca	Jan. 2003 (p. 54)	*The preproduction 98*
Moto storiche & d'epoca	Nov. 2003 (p. 18)	*The 200 Rally*
Motociclismo d'epoca	2 – 1996	*History of the Vespa*
Motociclismo d'epoca	4 – 1998	*The 125 with rod gear-change*
Motociclismo d'epoca	Dec. 1999 / Jan. 2000	*History of the 150 GS and impressions of riding it*
Motociclismo d'epoca	Nov. 2001 (p. 62)	*History of the Vespa PX*
Motociclismo d'epoca	Feb. 2002 (p. 22)	*The Russian Vyatka scooter, derived from the Vespa*
Motociclismo d'epoca	July 2002 (p. 70)	*The standard Vespa 125 Primavera*
Motociclismo d'epoca	Dec. 2002 / Jan. 2003 (p. 52)	*The Vespa 90 Super Sprint*
Ruoteclassiche	Dec. 1999 (p. 98)	*History of the 125 Primavera and the ET3*
Tuttomoto	Apr. 1995 (p. 98)	*Test of the Bajaj Chetak 150*
Tuttomoto	Jul. 1996 (p. 140)	*Article on the 90 Super Sprint*
Tuttomoto	Mar. 1997	*Comparison of the ET4 125 and other scooters with 4-stroke engines*

VESPA 400

To find out more about Charta, and to learn
about our most recent publications, visit

www.chartaartbooks.it

Printed in February 2006
by La Grafica - Cantù srl (Como)
for Edizioni Charta